CAN I SAY NO?

Stefanie Preissner, Munich-born but Mallow-raised, is the creator of hit comedy-drama series *Can't Cope, Won't Cope*. The show was originally commissioned by RTÉ but since then both seasons have been broadcast on BBC and acquired by Netflix.

Why Can't Everything Just Stay the Same?, her first book (published in 2017), was an Irish bestseller and nominated for an Irish Book Award.

She has also produced a series of short documentaries, *How To Adult*, with RTÉ Player.

Her one-woman theatre show, *Solpadeine Is My Boyfriend*, enjoyed sell-out runs in Dublin before touring internationally to Bucharest, Edinburgh and Australia, and – as a radio play – it became RTÉ's most downloaded podcast.

Stefanie graduated from University College Cork with a BA in Drama and Theatre Studies and Spanish. Alongside her career as a screenwriter and playwright, she has won several awards as an actor.

She is a regular contributor to Ireland's *Sunday Independent* newspaper and her voice is well-recognised from her prolific voiceover career. *Can I Say No?* is her second book.

She is currently working on more projects than she can cope with due to her ongoing battle with people pleasing.

She lives in Dublin and on Instagram @stefaniepreissner.

CAN I SAY NO?

ONE WOMAN'S BATTLE WITH A SMALL WORD

STEFANIE PREISSNER

HACHETTE
BOOKS
IRELAND

First published in Ireland in 2019 by
HACHETTE BOOKS IRELAND

1

Cataloguing in Publication Data is available from the British Library.

ISBN 978 1 4736 8789 9

Typeset in Arno Pro by redrattledesign.com

Printed and bound in Great Britain by Clays Ltd, Elcograf, S.p.A.

Hachette Books Ireland policy is to use papers that are natural, renewable and recyclable
products and made from wood grown in sustainable forests. The logging and manufacturing
processes are expected to conform to the environmental regulations of the country of origin.

Hachette Books Ireland
8 Castlecourt Centre
Castleknock
Dublin 15, Ireland

A division of Hachette UK Ltd
Carmelite House, 50 Victoria Embankment, EC4Y 0DZ

www.hachettebooksireland.ie

For Mam
Thank you for loving me whether I say yes or no.
I'm ferociously proud to be your daughter.

xx

Some of the names and details within the text have been changed to respect the privacy of individuals.

CONTENTS

Foreword

HAVE YOU EVER HEARD SOMEONE SAY THE FOLLOWING
SENTENCES?

1. I'm meant to be going out tonight, I hope they cancel.

2. It's easier to call in sick than ask for the day off.

3. I'm just not going to respond to that email until it's too late.

4. I'll say I'm on antibiotics.

Society has given us memes and unspoken etiquettes that

allow us to avoid having to say no. We have come up with the most inventive ways of declining, wriggling out, avoiding, hiding and negating without having to face the request and politely say, 'No.' Working out *how* to say no is a tricky business. I've tried many possibilities in my long battle of trying to escape being a yes-woman. I've been like a child jumping for joy when someone cancels the plans I was planning to cancel. I've been like that meme of the stressed woman standing in front of a whiteboard of algebraic equations as I realise I've run out of excuses. I've burned calories trying to run away from commitments I've made, all the while berating myself for not saying no in the first place.

For most of my life I was a bona-fide yes-woman. Apart from when I was a baby and *all* I said was no for about a month, there has always been a barrier between me and the word 'no'. A boundary, you might call it. But I wouldn't. Because having a boundary doesn't come naturally to me. It's a massive obstacle, my people-pleasing tendency. I've said yes to things that scared me, things that made me uncomfortable, things that I was fundamentally against. Now, I'm not saying I committed crimes or broke the law. I wasn't coerced into being a drug mule or anything. This isn't that kind of book. The scary things are more banal, like attending events I was uncomfortable at, singing for relatives at family events because I couldn't stand my ground, eating *cow-tongue*! That kind of thing.

Once I was sitting in my friend's house eating a bag of chips with salt and vinegar slathered all over them. Our hands were thick with grease and we were in our element.

My phone rang – WORK flashed up on the screen. (I use the term loosely: as you'll see later, I spent a lot of my twenties acting in terrible plays for no money.)

My friend said, 'Stef, you have to answer it.' I looked at my greasy hands and wanted to spare my phone screen and enjoy my chips but I answered it. Within an hour I was standing at the top of a ladder, hanging stage lights, still hungry and with a greasy screen.

So many memories of my friends and me don't have the endings I wish they had. So many are tinged with bitterness because I didn't know when to say no and call it a day. Now, I realise I'm at my best, my happiest, most serene, most charitable, fun, kind and joyous, when I am at my most uncompromising. 'No' is the biggest present I have ever given myself. But it's like gym membership or an Instant Pot cooker. It only works if you use it. My battle with 'no' is a daily one.

This book will look at how I learned to start saying no, in the same way I learned to quit smoking. One craving at a time. I'll chart my path of learning to say no and highlight some of the pitfalls and fears I faced in case you face the same ones. It will anticipate the worries and fears you may have: 'What if people are offended?', 'What if I have no friends?', 'What if I get no work?', What if people stop inviting me to things?' All the what-ifs. The answers will often be of the tough-love variety. The reality is that some people *will* dislike you for saying no ... but, really, those people are just boogers: it takes saying no to realise who your real friends, colleagues and champions are.

I recently spent some time with somebody's child. She's two and has no issue with saying no. This kid is inspiring in the same way any toddler is. She's never agreed to a proposal she hasn't liked. She knows only unconditional love. She has no idea that any other type of love exists. She hasn't had to change, adjust or manipulate anyone for anything. She smiles at people and they immediately smile back. In her whole life she has never had anyone not like her or not find her adorable. She has never had to do anything except be herself to please people. She has never been thwarted by someone's ulterior motives. She hasn't yet had to swap her desires for desirability. Watching her uncompromising requests being met with delight and charm gave me hope. I don't know when she will first encounter someone who demands that she adapt her nature to suit them. It won't be me. It will probably be some other child in some government-funded playground.

When I was leaving that kid, her granny invited her to wave goodbye to me at the door. She ran to the window before I'd even got my jacket. Social etiquette be damned. She didn't care that her enthusiasm to see me leave might be insensitive. Her thoughts were, You're leaving. I'm waving. It's lunchtime.

Then her granny suggested she give me a kiss to say goodbye.

'No.'

Simple. Clear. Boundary.

A boundary that many adults would force her to break. Not this adult.

She doesn't want to kiss someone she's only just met. And I think that's a lesson we could all benefit from.

The YESteryears

1

I DON'T KNOW WHEN I BECAME A YES-WOMAN. I CAN'T remember the first time I prioritised someone else's opinion of me over my own comfort. Maybe it was gradual, like growing out of my favourite dungarees.

If I was to pinpoint a pivotal moment in my yes-saying career, it was the summer between Second and Third Class when I was around seven. I spent all of my summers in Wexford with my nana. Nanas are notorious for being permission-givers. It's like they're incapable of setting boundaries for their grandkids. It's the best. Every time we went to Gorey to do the shopping, I'd get a ball. If it wasn't a ball it was a comic, or Pokémon cards, or a cream bun, or some new toy. Or sometimes all of the above. I didn't even have to convince her. It was just yes, yes, yes. A torrent of yeses rained down over our mobile home in Courtown, Co. Wexford, every summer.

As a kid, you can't understand the nuances of parenting. You can't see that your mother cannot be as lenient as your grandmother or you'd never stop watching TV and your teeth would rot from the sugar overload. It's all very black and white when you're a kid. I felt a deep love for Nana because she let me do whatever I wanted. Already the idea was forming in my mind that if you said yes to people, they would love you more. I loved people who said yes to me. Nana's yeses took us to great places. On our way to Gorey, we would stop to feed the ducks in some park outside Courtown. It was summer and we were time-rich. The days rolled out in front of us, displaying their offerings, like a man selling spices in an Arab souk.

I sipped TK lemonade in the Taravie hotel, my legs dangling off the high stool, I ate soup from a little metal bowl and my grandmother made eating scampi look elegant. I paid four pounds every other day to rent the same film to watch on the VCR in the mobile home: Nana knew I was a creature of habit and wouldn't force me to get a different one. It was usually *Casper* or *Annie* or, if I was feeling brave, *Hocus Pocus*. When my mam joined us for her two-week break, her vacation mode meant that the yeses kept coming. There was candy floss on demand, beach trips and 99s until I was sick.

There were hours I wouldn't see Mam's or Nana's face because their heads were buried in books as they waited for me to get tired of going on the waltzers or the bumper cars. They'd never make me get off. Summer was indulgent, abundant and just supreme. The warmth I feel thinking about it would melt even the coldest Mr Freeze ice-pop. I ate them too, until my tongue turned blue.

My first uncomfortable 'yes' happened on the beach. I hate the messiness of beaches. It would be great if there was no sand and the sea was warmer. But then it'd be a pool and there was no pool in Courtown at the time so most days my five friends and I ate our gritty sandwiches on the beach. I can't remember those girls' names – I knew them for only a summer – but at the time I thought they held the key to all the future doors in front of me. They were just girls around my age who were staying near my grandmother's mobile home. It was a tenuous connection at best, but when you're a kid, geography and age are the foundations of most friendships. That summer, and many summers since, I genuinely believed that if the 'in-crowd' didn't like me or approve of me, I would disappear into oblivion and be as irrelevant as the Polly Pocket I stopped playing with that summer because one of the girls told me they were 'for babies'.

I had been playing with those girls in the evenings on the caravan site. There was a version of a playground between the beach and the shop. All the kids hung out there but there wasn't much to do. The swings had been taken off their chains the year before because a child had broken his leg and the park got sued. Now we had a sort of dystopian playground framework to entertain us. The skeletal outline of the swing set was the backdrop to our evenings. Boys challenged each other to do chin-ups, girls curled their knees over the side bars and turned upside-down, their hair brushing over the worn, dusty earth, carved out by years of treading. It's a special kind of freedom, getting away from your life for a summer.

I had no way of categorising those girls. I had none of the information points I was used to having before judging someone's potential for friendship. Remember, I was seven! In Mallow, I knew what school you went to. If you went to my school, that was one link between us. I knew what sports you played, what grades you got, if you did your homework, if the teachers approved of you, if you always had a new pencil case in September. These are all salient indicators for a seven-year-old to make up their mind. I realised in Courtown that, without that information, I had to trust my own judgement of people and whether I wanted to be their friend.

This was empowering until I discovered the same applied to those girls choosing me as a friend. They didn't know I was a good student. They didn't know I was always on time, always had my homework done. They didn't know that I packed my schoolbag with my books in order of tallest to smallest, with my pencil case neatly tucked vertically down the side. I considered telling them I was good but, even at seven, I knew self-praise was no praise. They didn't have any endorsements to prime them to like me. I had to be my own endorsement. I had to be liked. But how?

It was an overcast day, but if Irish summer weather had been a deterrent we would never have left our mobile homes.

We layered up and ventured out, meeting, as we always did, by the giant anchor outside the Bosun's Chair restaurant at the entrance to the park overlooking the beach. I always wondered about the giant iron anchor we gathered around. It was over fifteen foot tall and cemented into the ground. It appeared to be some kind of nautical civic art, or maybe someone had left it there and, because it was too big to move, they just threw some cement around it to stop a lawsuit.

Anyway, giant anchors aside, nothing except a tropical storm would have changed our daily beach routine. In the nineties kids didn't have phones so we depended on our internal clocks to tell us how long was fair to wait for stragglers to join us. We waited for about twenty minutes. I was always the first to arrive, afraid that if I was late they wouldn't wait for me. I didn't want to give the girls an opportunity to leave me behind because, somewhere in my gut, I was sure that they would. I was first to arrive and last to leave. I didn't want to miss anything or leave room to be excluded from an in-joke. 'You had to be there' was the sentence I spent my childhood trying to avoid. I didn't trust that I would be included on my own merit, so I removed opportunities to be excluded as often as I could. After twenty minutes of kicking stones around and hanging off the giant anchor, we reckoned anyone missing had gone shopping or was doing errands with their family and we raced as a group down the dunes towards the sea.

That day, when we arrived onto the beach we saw we had to sit on the rocks because jellyfish had washed up on the shore. The strand looked like bubble wrap, with all the coagulated jelly scattered across the sand. I saw those polka dots as a clear warning sign that the water was not a place to be going in that day. I assumed we were all in agreement about avoiding the sea, but then the alpha girl, let's call her Alison, for the poetry of it, decided she wanted to go swimming. Swimming? Thousands of stinging creatures who had just come from the water were lying around warning us not to go in. But Alison was brave and bored. A dangerous combination. I started to panic. My insides resembled the jellyfish more than anything human. I looked around for a grown-up. Mam would definitely say no to this. We were unaccompanied. There was no lifeguard. Jellyfish were strewn across the beach, like sprinkles on an ice-cream cone, and whatever swimming acumen I had was certainly tailored to a pool rather than the sea. I immediately regretted my summer habit of having my swimsuit on under my clothes at all times.

I was nervous. The sea seemed to get very loud all of a sudden. I wondered if I picked up a shell and put it to my ear would I hear the disapproving, warning tone of my mother. What use would her disembodied warning be to me now that she was in Cork? I knew that saying, 'My mam won't let me,' would make me a laughing stock. If I refused on my own terms, I'd be exiled to the caravan park, cast aside, no longer invited to eat ice-cream on the beach, doomed to drift on the icy sea of loneliness for the rest of the summer. I imagined what the next day would look like if I said no. I had a vision of arriving to the anchor early and waiting for the others to appear as usual. I could hear the ticking clock in my head, time passing, while no one arrived. In this nightmare scenario the cool gang had arranged a new meeting place I didn't know about. They continued their summer happy and free while I befriended a fifteen-foot cast-iron anchor and found it comforting to know that it would always be there, sealed in cement. I had to say yes to be included, to be liked. I had to say yes to fit in. I had to say yes to survive this summer.

'Stefanie, are you coming in?'

'Ya, but you go first.'

Everyone started heading *en masse* in one direction, removing layers of clothing as they went. I was walking along with them but craning my neck behind me in the direction I wanted to go, which was away, away from the sea that was getting closer to us and us to it. But I couldn't turn the rest of my body and walk away from it. The only child in me was just too smitten at being part of a group, being 'in' with the cool girls. I wanted to belong more than I wanted to feel safe. I stood by the water's edge dragging out the minutes. If anyone was going to chicken out, I wanted them to do it before I got into the water. I waited for as long as I could, and when no excuse presented itself, when everyone was in and dunked and the hypothermic screaming was at its peak, I left my neatly folded clothes pile and walked into the sea.

I got in and under as fast as possible because, now that we were doing it, I had to make sure I got the full experience. I didn't want to give Alison the excuse to say, 'Oh, we all wet our hair but Stefanie didn't get that far.' I didn't want them all to get out before I was fully in and risk missing the full experience. We splashed around for a little while – I pretended I was swimming by bending my knees and letting the water come over my shoulders but my feet never left the seabed. I made sure I never got physically out of my depth. Emotionally, I was drowning in this people-pleasing sea of compliance.

For an only kid, it's hard to belong to a tribe. You spend so much time on your own, in your imagination or surrounded by adults. Feeling you're part of a group or that you belong in a casual, non-school environment is tough. Whenever I got the chance, though, it was a dragon I wanted to chase. Holidays, kids' clubs, playgrounds, birthday parties were my opportunities to soak up that feeling of belonging, value and worth. I made friends easily, which was a blessing and a curse. I would get attached very quickly by being nice and funny and agreeable, only to be devastated when the inevitable end came and the other kids had to go home. I had learned through repetition that the way to make friends was to be magnetic, to make people feel included, and to do what they wanted so they didn't go elsewhere to find a buddy. I was afraid that if I said no I'd never be asked to do anything again. I believed that each invitation led to the next and to say no would break the chain, shut the door and leave me trapped in a quarantine I couldn't escape from.

I believed I was more lovable with each yes. It was as though each yes I said, against my better judgement, was the next obliging rung on a ladder that would eventually lead to me being happy, whole and accepted.

This wasn't just a deluded perception I had in my childhood: it laid the foundation for an entire belief system, which informed my view of myself and the world well into my twenties. It can still pop up today, if I'm not careful.

If I don't take time to be mindful of my decisions and the motives behind my actions, this historical belief system lets me know that it is perfectly preserved inside me, like the ruins of Pompeii.

That day, I didn't get stung by any jellyfish, but the karma gods weren't going to let Alison get away with leading us all into a dangerous situation. She got stung on the leg, and in the midst of the consequent furore, I snuck away, back to Nana. I was totally part of the group now, which meant inclusion in every activity for the rest of the summer. Nana thought I was enjoying it. At the time I thought I was, too. She said yes to every sleepover offered. Every time one of the girls knocked for me she was there to grant permission. If she had said no, I would possibly have gone into a tailspin, fearing I'd be rejected or left out, but really I didn't want to go. I spent that summer, and most of my life, in the excruciating limbo of FOMO and FOBI. The Fear of Missing Out was always just that little bit stronger than the Fear of Being Included.

The great unknown that came with group activities, the anxiety around being out of my comfort zone and having to comply with other people's plans, would often keep me awake at night. I wandered around the caravan site eating Mr Freezes and bags of penny sweets the size of my head trying to work out if I'd rather go to Simon's birthday party all the way in Enniscorthy, when I didn't know what time we'd be home, what food we'd eat or what film we'd see, or would I prefer to stay on the caravan site by myself, and then have to listen to endless recounting of the night's events for the rest of the summer? It always came down to not wanting to be alone, not wanting to be the kid outside the in-joke. I was happiest with Nana, playing bingo or feeding ducks, but I knew that to have the option of company, I had to keep the invitations coming. Saying no would be closing a door I might never have the chance to open again.

We went to see *The Little Rascals*, in case you're wondering. As I sat in the dark, stuffing my face with popcorn, I knew before Alfalfa did that following his heart with Darla and saying no to the rules of the He-Man Woman-Haters Club was a bad idea. I tutted, 'I told you so,' as he wandered around, alone and friendless. The happy ending never reached me. I was too certain that bad things happen to people who go against their friends. The kid next to me wiped his nose with his hand, then asked if he could share my popcorn.

By the end of the summer I was craving the rules and boundaries of my home.

2

MY SCHOOL, LIKE MOST PRIMARY SCHOOLS, FUNCTIONED best when we, the students, adhered to blind and mindless conformity. There is a belief, probably a clause in some insurance policy, that no one is safe unless every child is abiding by every rule and every teacher and pupil agrees with the prevailing opinion on what is right. There is a sense of security and belonging available to children if they follow instructions and obey rules. If you do what you're told, you're elevated to the pinnacle of childhood approval.

I loved rules so I did what I was told, for the most part. I was 'good', my friends knew I was a 'good student', so their parents believed I was a 'good influence' on their child. My future prospects were thrown wide open because of my compliance. I was told I would 'do great things' and that I would 'go far' because I got full marks in my spelling tests. Each good result reinforced the mantra that I was valuable, worthy and inevitably successful because I was so good at following the rules and meeting other people's expectations.

My school, like any other, believed it was offering a sense of belonging and security with its rules. And, in a way, it was. It was nice to know that when the bell rang we all had to stand in a line. It was a small expectation that was easily met. There was a sense of achievement when the teacher praised us for being obedient – much like training puppies. In fairness, the line had its merit. There was sense to it being part of the routine. It meant we didn't bash into each other.

The line, or *líne*, to give it its Irish name and the word we used as we put our index fingers to our mouths as we stood in it, is a small example of the ways conformity helps to mitigate chaos where large groups of humans are concerned. Maybe that's why I find places like IKEA, airport security, book signings, Nando's or museums so comforting. All of those places have order. From being told which direction to walk in and which electronics go in which basket, to ordering your chicken wings and paying before you eat: I just love things to be clear and orderly, rules to be followed. If the rules are clear, even now, as an adult, I'm triggered into feeling 'good' and 'virtuous' when I follow them. That's how entrenched the early-years compliance lessons have become.

In school, the kids who broke the rules, climbed on tables, said bad words or didn't do their homework seemed dangerous to me. I was told they were going to be 'a bad influence'. To my childhood mind, their rebellion was liable to jump onto me if I got too close, like nits – which I was also super-wary of. The rebellion would spread like contagion until I, too, was seen as 'bad', someone people didn't want to be around. I tried to keep well away.

There was a girl in our class for a brief period – Blythe was her name. The kind teachers called her 'spirited'. The unkind ones called her 'a troublemaker'. I'm sure they used other names in the staffroom. Blythe found it really hard to obey rules. Maybe today she would have had a teacher's assistant with her in class but they didn't exist back then. Blythe couldn't or wouldn't stand in line in the yard. She couldn't or wouldn't stand and welcome the principal in Irish when she walked in. She didn't say prayers with us, didn't put her hand up. She distracted other students. My obedient friends and I were fascinated by her because, to us, Blythe was an anarchist.

More than any rule or lesson teachers could have taught us, Blythe existed to show us at first hand what happens to girls who don't blindly say yes. Her individualism and non-compliance with the prevailing ethos of the school made her an outcast. Blythe was quietly and subtly ostracised. She was left alone. I'm pretty sure it extended to her family. Her mother wasn't at the bake sales, her sister wasn't at the sports days. Looking back, she wasn't doing anything bad or evil, she just wasn't playing by the rules. She dared to colour outside the lines and play by her own rules. I didn't understand any of this at the time. Now, as a struggling yes-woman and people-pleaser, I think about Blythe often. And fondly. When I'm faced with a request I don't want to accept, or I'm struggling with a rule I can't see the point of – like taking your shoes off in someone's house – I think of Blythe and am certain she doesn't struggle in this way.

I didn't learn these lessons about conformity only through Blythe: they also came to me in the form of the Teenage Mutant Hero Turtles. 'They're called *Ninja Turtles*!' I hear you shout. Yeah, well, in Ireland in 1992, when I got Turtle-themed *everything* for my birthday, they were merely heroes, untrained in the ancient art of ninja. They didn't become ninjas in the UK or Ireland until the 2003 series. The UK broadcasters felt the word 'ninja' had connotations that were too violent for kids. Anyway, they still kicked ass. A recent buzz-feed quiz to find out 'Which Ninja Turtle Are You?' tells me that my adult self is most like 'Splinter'. He's the *sensei*, the leader, the master of all the Turtles. He's 'super-wise and mad-chill'.

I need a second opinion. As a kid I identified with Leonardo. According to the opening jingle of the cartoon, Leonardo is the leader. I didn't always feel like a leader but when I did lead, like the blue-masked Turtle, my orders were usually followed. He and I were both serious and might have had the phrase 'do-gooder' levelled at us. I like to think we both had an in-built sense of ethics. He seemed, reassuringly for me, as anxious as I was about rule-breaking and would often go to seek counsel from the wise Splinter when the way forward seemed unclear. Blythe was like Raphael: fierce, sarcastic and utterly unafraid. Blythe's signature red hairband matched Raphael's red mask and served as a traffic-light warning for me. If you say no to the status quo, you're trouble!

In my all-girls school, certain rules were like silk threads woven into the fabric of the place:

1. Be a good friend.

2. Be nice to everyone.

3. Share.

4. Be a good listener.

5. Be loyal.

6. Don't let people down.

7. Be a team player.

Those rules got in deep and proliferated like mushrooms in a damp carpet. Today I see the little fungi popping up again and again. It was a great way to promote kindness and goodness in our school but I wonder would I be a more confident, self-assured woman if those childhood rules had been different. I wonder if, in the boys' school across the road, where the rules were slightly different, they had the same 'laying the groundwork' impact as ours did for the now adult me. In the boys' school they had rules like:

1. No biting.

2. No kicking.

3. No hitting.

4. No spitting.

5. Obey your teacher.

6. Wash hands after using the toilet.

Those rules applied to us, too, but they weren't reiterated and hung on walls, like they were in the boys' school. Extra-curricular sports, like swimming, or birthday parties where we met our friends' brothers, highlighted the different approaches our schools took. The focus on non-violence indicated that, without the rule, boys would naturally tend that way. For us, the fact that a rule against it wasn't deemed necessary but that we needed to be reminded to listen differentiated us by gender from very young. Molecules of conformity were spritzed into the air in our classrooms by the cleaners at night. All day, I sat breathing in the fumes of this ethos. I soaked them up and they became part of me. I obeyed by being good, accommodating and nice. I was praised into being easy-going. In the presence of such power and authority I forgot I had my own. I didn't spit or bite or hit or kick with the same commitment I gave to being nice, a good listener and sharer.

At first, I struggled with sharing but that was stamped out of me as well.

Nothing got our class more excited than the Credit Union Christmas Colouring Competition, and 1995 was a particularly combative year. The picture to be coloured was a family of snowmen standing in the garden of a colonial house with snow falling on them. Question: Why are the houses that kids draw always those five-bed colonial mansions? No one in Mallow had one. We mostly lived in terraces, or bungalows or those two-storey houses where the roof is a scalene triangle, longer on one side. Trespassing accusations aside, we assumed the snowmen were built by the family who lived in the big house. Our teacher produced the A5 colouring sheets and gave one to each of us. I held mine with my arms outstretched and, if I had had the cultural reference maybe I'd have thought, This is how Michelangelo must have felt when he looked up at the ceiling of the Sistine Chapel. It was massive, and blank, and full of possibility.

The options excited my classmates and me. The buzzy thrill bubbled just below the level of frenzy for the afternoon. The teacher made sure it never spilled over into hysteria or 'hullabaloo', as she called it. Our desks were shifted out of their usual rows. We were allowed to work in 'clusters'. The change in format just added to the ceremony of the annual colouring competition. It felt like a treat. She played music. It was all new to us that year, the inaugural tradition. We weren't quite sure why we were allowed to have such fun without an obvious lesson being taught. I copped on pretty fast when the teacher gave her final instructions before letting us do our art.

'Now, girls, everyone is to put their colours in the middle of the cluster so each team can share.'

A lot of the class turned to look at me.

Oh, fuck. Oh, cluster fuck.

My mam owned a stationery shop at the time so everyone knew I had the best colours. And I knew that everyone else didn't have the necessary respect for stationery to be trusted with mine. The small voice inside me was screaming, 'STEF, SAY NO. GIVE THEM THE MARKERS BUT SAVE THE CRAYONS AT LEAST.' It was no use. The following few hours were Crayola carnage. It was a wax rendering of a murder scene. The girls got started and for a while I couldn't focus on my picture because I was so disturbed by what was happening. I'm sure being an only child and never having to share made the whole experience more acutely painful.

The music changed. 'Jingle Bells' was over. Jona Lewie piped up with 'Stop the Cavalry', a Christmas song that was originally a war song.

We were in the room. The music playing. That dead heat hung in the air. Its source, the massive oil radiators that clanged unexpectedly whenever they felt like it. Someone had had sandwiches with that luncheon meat with the face on it for lunch, and the smell hung in the air, along with spilled Capri Sun but no one seemed to notice. The ceilings were endlessly high, so high that halfway up the wall the colour changed so they'd only ever have to paint the lower half. Someone had stuck a dado rail around the boundary where the colour changed and called it a 'design feature'. I scanned the room for something to help me. Maybe there was a box of crayons somewhere I could swap out for mine. Our cluster was closest to the maths corner. Stacks of old copies of *Busy at Maths* were piled next to the abacuses and the folder of number lines, which would later be glued to the top of our desks. My eyes zoned in on the Trócaire box on the teacher's desk: maybe this was happening to me because I wasn't charitable enough and I was being punished.

Blythe was going too hard on my blue and I couldn't say anything. Jona was singing about having had enough and how he wished he was at home for Christmas – I don't think I've ever related to a song more. I just wanted to be at home, by myself, colouring . . . gently.

Blythe was demonically carving her way through the picture. The lines were furious and wild and she wasn't even *trying* to stay inside the lines. Little blue curls of crayon wax were scattered all over the page. It was like shrapnel after a bomb explosion. All my other crayons were going to be the same length but not the blue one. She was squeezing it so hard, totally concentrated, her face squished into a frown with exertion. She was like a dog that was going to overheat. The speed of her colouring and the heat from the strain was melting the crayon where she squeezed it. And I was meant to watch and share?

The teacher smiled at me. 'Good sharing, Stefanie.' I was confused but, I remember, kinda liking the praise. I took my favourite crayon 'Red Orange' and walked away from the cluster to the *bosca bruscair* with my pencil-parer. I pretended to pare my crayon. I was, in fact, saying goodbye.

*

The teacher gave me a sticker and a bun at the end of the day. My report said I was helpful and kind to other students. No one was any the wiser about the trauma the saga had caused me. I continued to be generous and share to get the buns. Once I did my friend's homework for her in exchange for a bag of Haribo.

The praise I received for sharing and being kind left a little imprint. It's a tiny stamp somewhere inside me that says, 'Stefanie is a better person because she let her friends ruin her stuff and didn't even cry.' I think one of the sins I told the priest during my first confession was that I was selfish. All because of the Credit Union Colouring Competition.

I coloured mine in perfectly. I used the white crayon – its only outing – and coloured each snowball individually. You couldn't tell they were coloured in unless you held it near the light, when the wax went shimmery. I was confident the judges would go to those lengths when assessing each of the individual renditions. I used Red Orange for the Christmas-tree baubles but 'Orange' for the carrot nose. I also made sure that I used a darker grey for the further away clouds and a lighter grey for the near ones to give perspective. I coloured the house in yellow, because there were no bricks in the walls: I assumed it was concrete and our neighbours had recently painted their house yellow so I thought it was trendy. I made little sprouts of grass spike up through the snow because in Ireland we never got complete coverage. I differentiated between the black for the coal and dark grey for the gutters. I did it perfectly. Not one millimetre outside the lines and as close to reality as you could hope for from a child.

And I still didn't win. Did they not hold it up to the light and see the white snowballs? Had I coloured in all that white for no reason? My friend Sarah added more snow and she didn't win. The girl who won coloured the snowballs blue. But snow is white? That's not right. Her poster was hung up in our local SuperValu for a whole month. Every time we went shopping I'd stare at it, hoping it would reveal itself to me like the Third Secret of Fatima. That girl had said no: no to the status quo, no to the rules, no to the institution. She'd stuck it to the man with her blue snowballs. I wonder where she is now. In my youth I thought of her sometimes – and wondered if her rebellion would land her in prison. It seemed like the inevitable resting place for someone so brazen as to say no to the universal rule that snow is white.

I wasn't an angel. I found outlets for breaking the rules. As an only kid, I got around sharing: I hid toys when kids came to play; I kept sweets in my jacket and turned into a 'pocket-muncher'. I remember at sleepovers the unkindness that exploded once a girl made a mean remark. That was all we needed to be cruel about someone who wasn't there. Maybe that's why girls are described as 'bitchy'. It's the opposite of our attempts to be nice and good.

The following year the competition rolled around again. The A5 sheets were handed out. They didn't feel so big this time. They weren't vast sheaves of freedom like they had been before. They were still just simple line drawings but now their whiteness was intimidating. It felt like a test. I was crippled by it. I would have preferred a paint-by-numbers or, even better, an already finished one where I could copy it perfectly, like the picture on a jigsaw box. There's no room for subjectivity with a jigsaw. You're right or you're wrong.

On Wednesdays in Fifth Class we played rounders. It was another masterclass in becoming a 'people-pleaser'. The lessons I was collecting as I ran from base to base were:

➤ Don't let your team down.

➤ Put your teammates ahead of you as an individual.

➤ Obey the rules.

➤ Don't cry.

➤ And, as always, be nice to everyone.

I learned these rules all together and in one day.

I had always suffered with exercise-induced asthma. If my body suspected that anything close to exercise was happening, my little bronchioles would act up. It wasn't as debilitating as it sounds – I just made sure to carry my inhaler wherever I went. I quite enjoyed rounders so I was more than happy to suck on my Ventolin and avoid my rattling lungs. It had become normal for me to take the medication to allow me to abide by the school rules. I wouldn't speak up when I was getting 'chesty', I'd just take my inhaler. That's probably why, on that one Wednesday, I thought speaking up would be seen as non-compliant, or have made me seem like a difficult kid.

During our first game of rounders that day Clare, a super-athletic and driven girl, grabbed the bat out of my hands, even though it was my turn. I wanted to grab it back but I also wanted to be good. I knew that by sharing, which, clearly, she was not doing, I was better than her in the eyes of the teacher. I didn't complain. Just after she pulled the bat out of my hand I stood with my arms by my sides, calculating how many Brownie points I would get, waiting for the teacher to praise me when – BANG! Tennis ball straight into the temple. I had a massive bruise on my face. If I'd been able to stop myself crying I would probably have scored even more Brownie points for being brave or 'a trooper', but I couldn't. The tears streamed down my face and left little drop marks on my runners. I got a lot of praise and attention because I'd been injured in the act of sharing – I felt like an even better person than a non-injured sharer would have been. I got another bun. The teacher asked me if I was OK in a way that answered the question for me: 'It's not sore any more, sure it's not?' and 'You're all right, aren't you?' All the time I was learning: don't tell the truth, don't speak up, just be OK. Don't make a scene and you'll be more likeable and accepted. At all costs, don't be who you really are.

The positive reinforcement that went along with self-sacrifice was powerful. Saying yes to things you really didn't want to say yes to, like having your property destroyed or getting a black eye, were rewarded. 'Good sharing, Stefanie. Sorry about the shiner. Here's fifty grams of sugar and butter.'

You have to say yes to other people's priorities. You have

no choice. You have to kiss and make up with someone even if you feel put down or humiliated by them. You can't make mistakes. Compliance is better than honesty. Anger is not allowed. You have to smile while you cry and say you're OK. Being a victim gets you positive attention. I became a master at ignoring my true feelings and replacing them with others that were more appropriate and palatable. I was a co-operative ninja: skilled in the ancient art of not causing a scene, adept at being good-natured, and well on my way to being a benevolent, congenial member of society.

I became so skilled at replacing my true feelings with more appropriate ones that eventually, years later, I came to realise that I didn't know my true feelings any more. Like those children who stop crying because they know no one is listening, my feelings stopped making themselves known because what was the point? This habit of overriding my instincts and emotions followed me through life.

The endless yeses, compliance and people-pleasing wore me down until I was like the stump of my blue crayon. Blunt, stunted and melted where I had been squeezed. Looking back now, I feel there was a key lesson I was not taught in school. Sharing your things freely and easily is good but that shouldn't equate to giving yourself freely and easily. You don't have to *be* the blue crayon. You just have to give it.

While writing this, I googled 'Who was the first martyr?' I thought it'd be clever to make some tenuous connection between myself and someone who has famously 'taken one for the team'. St Stephen was the first martyr. My namesake. I'M LITERALLY NAMED AFTER THE FIRST EVER CHRISTIAN MARTYR. FML. I had no chance, really.

3

IT WAS AROUND THAT TIME, AFTER THE ROUNDERS
debacle, that I began to notice how often I would avoid saying
no. Sometimes I would swallow the word. Other times a little
voice was saying I didn't want to do something or had noticed
someone else making a mistake. I had learned, somehow, that
no one likes a precocious child who points out the mistakes
of others, even if she is correct in saying it's not pronounced
'supposably'.

Years later I was watching an episode of *The Simpsons*, one
of the 'Treehouse of Horror' episodes, and Lisa Simpson,

dressed in a pointy black hat, said, 'Why is it when a woman is powerful and confident they call her a witch?' It got me thinking. In my early years I took a lot of lessons from Lisa Simpson but unfortunately they may not have been the most helpful for me to learn.

I grew up watching *The Simpsons*. I adored it. I watched little Lisa as I aged and she didn't. I saw her stand up against every terrible thing she encountered, from bullying and sexism to corporate greed and racism. I learned new phrases like 'cesspool of corruption' from her and had my way of thinking changed. She was smart, ambitious and driven. She had empathy and integrity and kindness. As I describe her now, she was almost the perfect role model for any young girl growing up – a talented saxophonist, who got good grades. And yet the main thing I learned from Lisa was how *not* to be her. Why? Because *The Simpsons*, as a TV show, seems to have hated Lisa and continually punished her for the characteristics I've mentioned above. She is ostracised and teased for being smart and ambitious. Other characters laugh at her and roll their eyes.

Among my childhood friends it wasn't cool to like Lisa – she wasn't the character to aspire to. Lisa Simpson was a fable, a cautionary tale of what happens to whistleblowers and girls who speak up. Better to say nothing and be accepted than to be a lonely Lisa Simpson. Each time Lisa speaks up about terrible role models for young girls, like the blonde Malibu Stacey doll, or becoming vegetarian for ethical reasons, or equal rights for the kids in her school, she is met with failure. In one episode, 'Lisa vs Malibu Stacey', Lisa is playing with her dolls and becomes disillusioned with the pre-programmed phrases spouting from them. Bart laughs at her concerns. She responds:

'It's not funny, Bart. Millions of girls will grow up thinking that this is the right way to act . . . that they can never be more than vacuous ninnies whose only goal is to look pretty, land a rich husband, and spend all day on the phone with their equally vacuous friends talking about how damn terrific it is to look pretty and have a rich husband!'

Lisa delivers this little speech in a way that makes her seem hysterical. It sets her up as a fundamentalist on a tyrannical mission. At the end of the episode, when the doll she has voiced with more progressive phrases fails to sell, the viewer feels the status quo has been reinstated by her failure. For Lisa to progress, be successful and change the minds of the people around her is impossible. As a kid, I learned that if I spoke up, like Lisa, I would be casting myself in the role of the shrill annoying secondary character, who would inevitably fail to get where she wanted to go. So I stayed quiet. In one episode she changed herself entirely during a summer beach holiday and was popular, cool and accepted.

I had had a taste of that freedom from my summers in Courtown – the ability to be free of the identity you have in your home town. The way to be loved, popular and accepted was to change myself to fit in. That meant being agreeable, and if I couldn't say yes, I should say nothing at all and let other people join the dots. As Bart sings to Lisa when she tries to convince others to become vegetarian too: 'You don't make friends with salad.'

I worked hard to hide any salad-type opinions or desires. Even saying no to a simple question became something to avoid. One time, at my friend Tom's house, we were playing with Power Rangers. I was more of a Polly Pocket kid but having a playmate was the ultimate goal and made the choice of toy less important. I needed to go to the toilet at Tom's house. I stood up, put my red Power Ranger on a little table and told Tom I would be back momentarily. 'Do you know where the toilet is?' he asked.

I remember feeling silly, like I had felt when we had to paint pictures of Humpty Dumpty in Senior Infants. Every child in the class painted a picture of an egg on a wall and I painted one of a boy. Everyone laughed because I didn't know Humpty Dumpty was an egg. How was I meant to know? Where in the song does it say he's an egg? It doesn't. How did they all know and I didn't? Had I missed a memo?

As I stood in Tom's bedroom with an increasingly full bladder I wondered, yet again, if I had missed a memo. I reckoned that Tom would only ask me if I knew where the bathroom was if I was supposed to know already. If I wasn't meant to know, surely he'd just tell me how to get there. The directions weren't forthcoming so I decided I should know. I left his room and wandered around the hallway. The house had a vaguely similar layout to my aunt's so I opened the door of what would have been her bathroom and discovered Tom's mother brushing her hair. I bolted away and, with the time that had elapsed since I'd first had the impulse to go to the toilet but said nothing, I wet myself. I spent the rest of the day mortified and trying to make sure Tom's sister's tracksuit pants didn't fall down.

It was such situations that made the idea of sleepovers a living nightmare for me. Once, my friend Emer invited me to a sleepover, along with everyone else in the class. I didn't want to go but I didn't want to be left out. What would happen if everyone in the class was hanging out without me and something occurred to bind the group together without me? What if I came to school on Monday and they had invented a new game on the night and I couldn't play? What if, what if, what if? I couldn't risk that sort of social suicide. It was the same fear I'd had all those years ago on the beach in Courtown. The same fear of being 'other', of being left behind because I refused to go with the flow. I didn't say no, and I attended the sleepover. You could argue that by attending, I said yes, but I see it as an unspoken no: a no I should have said.

The boys in my life didn't seem to have the same fears. Tom would often miss parties or choose a family event over a trip to the circus with his friends. He didn't seem fazed in the slightest about what would happen without him. He couldn't have cared less. From the inside, I could see that no one was gossiping about him in his absence, there was no conspiracy around his exclusion, but I couldn't take those facts and apply them to myself.

That sleepover was the first of many I should have said no to. During the evening, somewhere between playing Twister and Kitchen Dares, someone asked me if I'd kissed a boy. For what felt like years I had to keep up the pretence that I had – 'Mike who went to another school'. That boy saved me in many ways but it was one of the most energy-draining relationships, in terms of upkeep, I've ever had. I created something from nothing. Out of thin air, I summoned a fake boyfriend. With that simple yes, I undermined myself and my reality. Telling the truth wasn't enough. Stefanie who told the truth, who answered, 'No,' was less-than: she was less interesting, less popular, less worthy, less cool, less valuable than the Stefanie who lied and said yes.

After the Truth or Dare section of the sleepover we moved into the kitchen. Kitchen Dares was an awful game: two people went into the kitchen, unattended, and created a cocktail of anything from tinned tuna and MiWadi with an egg yolk to condensed milk with Tabasco and corn flakes. You were dared to drink the whole thing down and you couldn't say no. I'll always remember the girls who made up stories about being allergic or having coeliac disease to get out of having to drink the kitchen dare. No one believed them and they became contemptible for being bad sports. You don't make friends with salad and you certainly don't make friends with fake coeliac disease.

I downed my egg yolk concoction and managed to pretend it 'wasn't that bad'. The next day I cried to my mother about a tummy-ache. She assumed it was from overdosing on chocolate or ice-cream the night before. Little did she know I might have had salmonella from the raw egg and spices I'd downed in the name of popularity and acceptance.

If it's hard to say no to your peers, it's nigh on impossible to say no to your teachers. I realised this around Easter when I was in Fifth Class. When it came to casting the Easter play, a dramatic retelling of the death and resurrection of Christ, I didn't say no to being cast as Pontius Pilate. I had to stand in front of the whole school and the parents, dressed in a white sheet with half a football on my head, adjudicating the trial and crucifixion of whichever girl was cast as Jesus. I should have said no from the start but I *definitely* should have said no when my favourite teacher asked me if I had a Pontius Pilate costume at home. I mean, *who* has that? What kind of nine-year-old has the outfit of a first-century Roman governor of Judaea in their dress-up box? But I wanted to be the best. I wanted to be her favourite in the class. I wanted the super-speller stickers and the gold stars and the pats on the head, so I said yes. My no, yet again, went unspoken.

I decided, in my infinite wisdom, that he probably wore a skull cap, like the pope (he didn't). I got a cheap yellow football in the toy shop, cut it in half, turned it inside out and put it on my head. As I stood in front of my school throwing the opening salvos that would lead to the inevitable death of Our Lord and Saviour, I understood, on a new level, Judas's betrayal of Jesus. Except I was Judas and Jesus in one. With half an inverted football on top.

I held tight to the belief that I was more valuable to my school, to the cast of my play and, in a way, to the world because I was more easy-going.

I was still a child. I hadn't worked out a coping mechanism to deal with disappointing someone by not doing what they want. I know now that there's a moment of discomfort when you draw a line in the sand. It's that feeling at the end of a therapy session when the therapist asks for the money. It's the moment at the end of a date when you know it hasn't gone well and you have to find a way to wrap it up. It's the moment your friend comes out of the dressing room in a terrible outfit and it's your turn to speak. It's wriggly and gross to speak the truth, and when I was nine the discomfort made it impossible. At some point in primary school, my desires became less important to me than my desirability.

From then on, the word 'no' became like the lyrics to 'Macarena'. I knew it existed, I could hear it, there was a dance routine around it . . . but could I say it?

No.

I danced the dance and muttered the guttural sounds to the Spanish pop song. I was delightful, I was popular, I was good and I was up for anything.

One time, I was asked if I liked dogs. The truth was that I hated dogs. Well, I didn't hate them but I hated how I felt around them. I hated the sweaty palms and the tight chest, the panic that would descend upon me whenever I got near a dog. I didn't say any of this in response to the question. I didn't say anything. I didn't feel I was allowed to say I was afraid of dogs. If I wasn't allowed to *say* I was afraid, was I allowed to *be* afraid? This is where it all gets dark and messy and dangerous.

4

THE ISSUE WAS THAT IN REALITY AMONG HER PEERS, young Stefanie acted if she was up for anything. I was so far from agreeable and easy-going. Going contrary to my nature all the time meant that I was a really anxious child. Always putting myself in situations I would rather avoid took its toll. I was constantly wrapped in a film of terror. I felt stripped of all agency and control because I constantly had to say yes. I compensated by being excessively controlling about anything I *could* control.

I kept my room spotless.

My books were laid out on my shelf in order of height and thickness.

My Beanie Babies were organised in a pyramid with the bigger ones at the bottom, the pile topped off with my favourite plush lobster.

Everything was neat and clean and orderly.

My room, my environment. My way.

I had to have my socks smooth on my legs, no scratchy seams or bunching fabric. Clothes had to be soft, no wool or anything itchy touching my skin. My vegetables had to be dried on a sheet of kitchen paper before they were served up to me because I hated 'wet things' on my plate. My school books had to be covered perfectly in clear film. No bubbles. My mother spent hours every September smoothing the clear plastic over the latest edition of *Busy at Maths* with a credit card to get rid of air pockets. If there was any control I could have, I had it. My mother should be sainted.

Meanwhile, outside my comfort zone I was gathering those gold stars and pats on the back. All of my self-compromising yeses were rewarded. The praise I was receiving for being a yes-woman was a highly addictive drug. When I said yes to things I didn't want to do, I could bask in the approval and validation I got from being compliant. Every day some act of agreement or compliance was rewarded, most often with food, praise or laughter – three of life's most addictive things.

Of course, personality type is a key factor in becoming a yes-woman. Certain people, mainly those who derive pleasure from and are energised by socialising and adventure, find it easy to say yes to spontaneous suggestions. Those extroverts thrive in situations I find chaotic. In school, highly structured, with clear rules, and strictly timetabled, I could simulate extroversion. I knew how to make my friends laugh by pushing (but never crossing) the boundaries with teachers. I knew that volunteering to read aloud would get me Brownie points with the teacher, while putting on a funny voice or deliberately mispronouncing a word would score me cool points with the girls. I got away with making the occasional quick-witted but vaguely inappropriate comment to the teacher because my grades were high and I was respectful. I was good most of the time and always well-behaved when it mattered, so teachers overlooked the odd offence that made me an exciting, even thrilling, friend to have around. I entertained because I appeared unpredictable but I worked to a very simple formula. Be good more often than not, and always when adults are stressed. Outside that, there's wiggle room for popularity.

Even an introvert like me can have periods of extroversion. But time spent socialising or being gregarious has opposite effects on introverts and extroverts. I see myself as a candle with a small flame. When I am being extrovert, that candle is taken into the wind: I become diminished to an ember and need to retreat to a quiet refuge to rebuild myself until I am a full flame again. Extroverts are fuelled by being around other people. They replenish their energy stores by engaging with other people.

In school, introverts are often mistaken for being good because they are quiet. They cause no trouble and have labels like 'studious' or 'hard-working' attached to their report cards by teachers. In my school these were not the words the kids used: they swapped them for crueller synonyms, like 'swot' or 'teacher's pet'. I learned quickly that I couldn't give in to my full introvert if I wanted to have a big circle of friends.

I grew up watching the American kids' TV show *Sister, Sister* on Nickelodeon. It was completely engrossing – a whole thirty minutes would pass in an instant. The series tracked the lives of identical twins Tia and Tamera after they were reunited in a shopping centre having been separated at birth. The twins and their single parents moved in together, spending each episode getting to know each other and realising how different the twins were in spite of looking the same. For the first four seasons the song underscoring the opening credits was about how the girls 'never knew how much I missed ya' and how, now that they had found each other, they were 'never letting go'. At Season Five, though, the jingle changed. I had just moved into First Year of secondary school when it was broadcast in Ireland. After school one day I turned on the TV to watch the latest offering and felt totally thrown when I couldn't sing along as I always had. Suddenly the lyrics were about how the sisters each had their own lives and their own style and everyone one was noticing how different they had come to be.

My discomfort waned as I listened to the new words and a sense of calm descended on me. The twins were going to start doing their own thing, not just undermine their own comfort for the sake of the other. The good-at-school twin, Tia, was always anxious when Tamera would concoct a notion that inevitably broke some rule or took them out of bounds. By the same token, Tamera's controlling, tidy and scheduled life made Tia feel like a caged animal. As the purple background flashed, signalling the end of the opening credits, instead of tossing my backpack with my completed homework in it towards the front door for the morning, I took out my copy book and sat poised to take notes.

Well, I didn't actually do that. What twelve-year-old takes handwritten notes from a beloved TV show? But I did watch with an attention to detail that is now reserved for Mam in the kitchen. I try to learn from her by watching how she manages to chop an onion so finely. That keen observational eye was the lens through which I watched Season Five of *Sister Sister*.

From time to time, the show would 'break the fourth wall': Tia or Tamera would look right into the camera and speak to the audience. When they did this at the start of Season Five, explaining into the lens that they were moving into separate bedrooms, I felt they were speaking directly to me. I knew it was important for me to watch closely. I had always longed for a twin. When I was small and adults asked me, 'What do you want to be when you grow up, Stefanie?' I used to say, 'A twin'. I thought I would be unconditionally accepted and loved, eternally cherished and appreciated if I had someone I'd shared a womb with. Maybe, I thought, if I could have a biological other half, they would never require me to be anything other than my true self.

Seeing Tia and Tamera love each other *and* acknowledge that they needed space from each other because they were so different was a wild concept for me. Having space away from someone was always confusing. I thought if you were alone it was the same as being lonely, lost or abandoned, but through the show I was realising that having your own space was a gift. I was going out of my way to please people so I would never be alone, but now, I discovered, it was less like solitary confinement and more like the delicious moment when you get to starfish in a double bed having been curled up next to your friends on a sleepover. As I watched that day, the wild concept was forming in my head. I had taken the first step in realising I was not being true to myself in trying to be liked by everyone I met.

At some point, late in primary school, it got too hard to keep up the constant compliance. We were growing older so there were more offers of parties, sleepovers, holidays and weekends with other people's parents.

Laura was having a sleepover for her tenth birthday. We were all going to bring a sleeping bag and watch a horror film. Jessica said her sister had one on video and she would sneak it to the party because Laura's parents wouldn't let her rent anything more than a 12-rated movie from Xtra-vision. The horror film was actually my idea. I was very enthusiastic about planning these events. It was all just mighty while they were hypothetical, but once the reality was in front of me, I fell to pieces. I had been coming home telling Mam all these great plans for the party: we were going to crimp each other's hair, melt marshmallows on the fire and do face masks. We were so grown-up now that skin care had to be part of any group activity. My mother couldn't have known that I didn't want to go. *I* didn't even fully know.

My stomach was telling me, though. I had what I call

'worry pains'. It's the pain in your stomach that you get when you're anxious about something but you're not quite sure what it is. It's the pain I get now when the envelope with the harp comes through the door or when I have five missed calls from anyone in my family.

If I had said no to Laura, she would have been crushed. She'd made me feel like a key part of the thing. I had been crucial in its design and without me it couldn't be executed. It was like this party was our child, and if I said no I was abandoning her and it. Part of me enjoyed feeling special and needed. I went. The day and the evening were OK. There were enough activities, cake, hair crimpers and dance routines to keep me distracted. The problem came when it was time for bed. I got sleepy before some of the other girls, halfway through the horror film, which I didn't find scary. (Gotta keep some semblance of street cred here, OK?) My eyes got heavy and so did my stomach. The worry pain was back with a bang.

I went to the bathroom. Nothing. I was in there for ages but deep down I knew this was not a digestive issue. There's no greater hell than being in someone else's house, in their bathroom, feeling unwell, knowing someone else needs to use the toilet and not knowing what to do. Eventually Laura called her mum. I remember her in her nightie, her gentleness and warmth, as she stroked my hair. She asked me if I wanted to go home. I shook my head. I didn't want to be any trouble. I didn't want to be the difficult one. She must have had a sixth sense because she stopped asking me and just told me she was going to call my mother.

Mam picked me up. I cried the whole way home, tears of

disappointment in myself. I was disappointed that I hadn't been able to stay at the party. I was disappointed that I wasn't the kind of person who wanted to stay at the party. At the time, I didn't understand why I was different from the other girls. I didn't understand why I didn't want to stay at the party. Words like 'introvert' and 'extrovert' hadn't reached me. Buzzfeed hadn't been invented to tell me which personality type I was. Now I realise I didn't want to stay at the party because there were too many unknowns. Which bed would I sleep in? What if I had a worry pain? What if I woke up before everyone else? Would I have to lie still in the bed and wait? What if I got hungry? What time would Mam collect me? WHAT IF I WET THE BED?

I couldn't cope with all of the unknowns, and I was even worse with the knowns. I knew the moment would come when I got tired, but the first person to fall asleep was always seen as the wuss. I knew the food provided wouldn't be enough and would probably be served in 'sharing bowls', which meant trying to split them in unspoken diplomacy. I knew the chat would get into boy territory too quickly. I knew I had to be on my guard so I didn't let any hints of discomfort or childishness peek through. That meant denying fear of horror films, belief in Santa or being baffled by the details of menstruation.

It was exhausting having to keep your guard up for that long. I was disappointed that I hadn't been able to say no in the first place. I was disappointed in everyone else that they were enjoying themselves, or able to pretend they were, without having to go home. My mother was disappointed in herself for putting me through the whole thing.

'I thought you wanted to go.'

'I didn't! Why did you let me?'

'You seemed really excited about it.'

'I wasn't!'

'But you helped Laura plan it.'

'Yeah, but I didn't think it would actually happen.'

'Well, it's over now. You're OK, aren't you?'

'Ya.' Then a pause as a horrific realisation hit me: someone else was going to turn ten and have a sleepover next week and the week after and, like Sisyphus, I was now doomed to push a boulder of a sleeping bag up a hill for eternity.

I started crying again.

I know now that situations like this, where I'm out of my comfort zone, are difficult – and, hey, it's not my fault. It's my personality type: I don't enjoy overnight group activities – and that's fair enough. Now, as an adult looking back, I'm aware that, statistically, there must have been other girls in my class, and possibly at that sleepover, who were introverts, who also found that party a little overwhelming but felt they couldn't leave for fear of missing out. How different things might have been if I had found a kindred spirit in my childhood. But that would have been possible only if I had known I was an introvert, and I didn't.

That night I worked out a code with Mam. We decided that if I ever said, 'So-and-so wants me to . . .' while asking for permission to do something in front of them, she was immediately to say no. This abdication of responsibility from me to my mother allowed me to remain 'up for anything' and 'great fun'. The first time we used it, it worked perfectly. I was anxious my mother wouldn't remember our conversation because I was asking in front of my friend's mum.

Amy was one of the kids I spent the most time with growing up. She lived on the street where my childminder was and her mum and mine were besties. She was a year younger than me, and although that usually prohibits any kind of friendship when you're nine, we saw past it and hung out all the time. Amy was super-athletic. She played camogie, did swimming, gymnastics and could climb the Three Trees on our green faster than any of the boys. I loved losing track of time and getting grazed knees with Amy. I did not like organised team sports. Playing rounders or tip-the-can on the green was fine but I did not want to go to some benighted gym hall and have a grown-up blow a whistle at me to make me 'go faster'. Amy wanted me to join camogie. We'd played all day – I used her brother Billy's hurley, which was basically a tennis racket it was so huge, so I was at an unfair advantage. I hit every ball that came my way with ease. Amy, being only eight, just saw the balls flying into our home-made goalpost and decided I needed to join.

To Amy and everyone on the green, I was a likeable, popular girl, who they wanted to play with in formal settings too. That felt great. But I did not want to chase that feeling to the town park where they played Gaelic Games.

Mam came to collect me from my childminder, Amy running over to the car. Her mum was in the background. I was racing to get to the car before the deal was sealed.

'Can Stef come to camogie at seven? She's really good!'

My mam looked to Amy's mum, with a raised eyebrow that

asked, 'Is she really? Or am I wasting my money on another thing she'll ditch as soon as she has to be outside in the rain?'

Amy's mum nodded. 'They've been playing all day.'

I arrived, breathless. 'Mam! Mam. AMY WANTS ME TO JOIN CAMOGIE TONIGHT.'

'What? Breathe. You'll give yourself an asthma attack.'

'Amy. Wants me. To join camogie.'

My eyes were wild, feral, full of fear, trying to communicate with my mother.

(Actually, it was probably a lot less subtle than I thought it was at the time. I'd say Amy's mum was definitely on to us.)

Mam caught my eye. I thought I saw her wink but I probably imagined it. Maybe it was an exhausted twitch. Maybe it was a glint. Maybe it was all the goals I would never score for Mallow United flashing through her eyes. Whatever it was, my mam and I were on the same wavelength.

'No, Stef. You can't do camogie. It'll clash with speech and drama in the winter.'

Solid response.

Amy and I did a ceremonial wail of disappointment, then quickly got over it.

Mam and I drove home, thrilled with our new code.

I had found a way to be a likeable, popular girl, with a mother who wouldn't let me do any of the things I secretly hated doing.

That little set-up with Mam made me feel safe. Recently I spent time with a friend who has a three-year-old. The kid is transitioning from the potty to the toilet, and whenever he needs to go and they're in company, he'll say, 'Mum, can you help me with my buckle?' He doesn't wear a belt or anything resembling a buckle but in this way he can ask for help without embarrassment. The fact that there's nothing embarrassing about needing your mother or help is beside the point. It was for me, too. As a kid, I didn't want to face the moment of discomfort that comes after saying no to someone. There's a millisecond of disappointment that flashes across someone's face when you tell them you're not going to fulfil their request, meet their demand, accept their offer or grant their wish. It's like in the Simpsons when Bart slows down the recording of Lisa breaking Ralph's heart by rejecting him and the whole event plays out one millisecond per hour and you 'can actually see the moment his heart breaks'. Even now I hate that moment. I avoid it when I can but if I can't I just endure it. Back then, having Mam say no for me was my saving grace.

5

SECONDARY SCHOOL DIDN'T HAVE THE GROUP TABLES or enforced sharing of stationery but it was still a cluster fuck. In secondary school you start adding free will, independence and hormones into what is already a swirling vortex of confusion and emotions.

The school part of secondary education was great. The rules were clear. I knew exactly what to do to be a good student. The teachers were honest and frank about how they could be won over. Be on time, shut up, and get good grades in their class. That I could do. Except maybe the shut-up part, but Meatloaf sang it and I lived it. Two out of three ain't bad. Unless you're a perfectionist.

The social part of secondary school was a whole other story. We were that bit older so our parents and teachers had given us more freedom and agency. This happened around the fourth year and suddenly we were expected to make our own decisions, develop a moral compass, know how to measure consequences and outcomes, but still we had to eat our vegetables and be home by ten.

The collective loosening of the parental reins among my peers meant that friends became more important than parents. It was now your friends who were the yardstick and rubric of what was acceptable. Except acceptable was just called 'cool' and that definition changed daily. Some kids loved the freedom. I didn't feel safe in this new paradigm. Why couldn't we let the grown-ups stay in charge? Your parents are always your parents but your friends can drop you. You have to earn your friendships and work to maintain them. You have to stay on the right side of your friends, always keeping them happy.

Now I know this is a dysfunctional way of looking at friendship but I'd seen it with Blythe and many fallen comrades since her.

I continued to watch *Sister, Sister* after school most days. I watched the twins differentiate a little more from one another, assisted by their separate bedrooms. The need to take notes was getting stronger. It kept coming back to the same thing for me: I could never work out if I was Tia or Tamera. Tia was honest, responsible, mature and usually got straight As; she did better at school than her twin. Tamera was impulsive, spontaneous and seen to be the more 'fun-loving' of the pair. During my teenage years, the me who clowned around in class making people laugh – I was more overtly like wild Tamera. I once hid in a cupboard for an entire biology lesson, and there was the time I made a friend punch me in the face because I wanted a black eye and she was caught by a teacher.

The difference was that Tamera seemed to enjoy the antics: she would thrive on the excitement while I experienced adventure like the lifecycle of a star speeded up. BANG! A star is born and there's loads of energy and excitement until it fades and dies. It wasn't just emotional exhaustion: I spent most of my childhood on antibiotics and steroids for acute chest infections. I couldn't sustain the 'giddy twin' persona for very long but I was afraid of being too like Tia. People rolled their eyes and called her a 'party-pooper'. She was the parent type with her friends, always highlighting the trouble they could get into, worrying about the outcome. If something exciting was happening people wanted Tamera there, not Tia.

All of the yeses I was doling out in school with my friends – the rule-breaking, the cinema trips I didn't want, the sleepovers, permanent-marker tattoos and secret handshakes – meant that whenever I could say no safely, I said it. It's the reason parents all over the world have near-breakdowns when their kids become teenagers. The teens are out in the world trying to be good and accepted, and keep in with their friends, so their cynical, negative side needs an outlet and home is the only safe place, for most people. Exhausted from pleasing people around us, the noes get stored up for home time.

I've said it before and I'll say it again. My mother should be sainted. Maybe all mothers should be. The obstacle course of teenage adolescence is horrific when you're going through it – but have you ever watched the TV game show *The Cube*? If so, you'll know the frustration of watching the contestant trapped inside a Perspex box, repeating the same mistakes over and over and you're screaming at the television, 'THIRTY-FOUR, GOD DAMN YOU! THERE ARE THIRTY-FOUR SQUARES ON THE FLOOR!' That's what I imagine parenting is like. They can see that there are thirty-four squares on the floor because, like the home-viewer, they have a different perspective. They have an aerial view. Meanwhile we teens are down on the floor, counting and recounting squares, trying to look cool, aloof and not humiliate ourselves in front of our friends. We are trapped in a Perspex box of emotion and hormones, and someone shouting the answer to us would disqualify us, make us appear incompetent and prove our lower status. It's no wonder that when your parent mentions you've left your zip open after you've spent a day with your friends they get twenty-four hours' silent treatment.

The issues I had at home as a teenager, like feeling misunderstood and unappreciated, were less about my mother not knowing me and more about my own uncertainty about who I was. At school, with all the personal compromises, all the yeses, I was struggling to develop a sense of identity. Other kids were testing things, developing tastes and a sense of self, and I was just taking on the identities they were forming. On a weekend Sally, Mary or Jane would go to the city with their parents to shop for clothes. They'd try on fifteen outfits and come back with the perfect trendy ensemble. I'd see their new Hobo hoody or their Buffalo boots and the following week I'd be dragging my mother from shop to shop to find that *specific* hoody or those *exact* shoes. It was the difference between casually browsing a shop and assiduously hunting for particular items. There was nothing casual, laid-back or enjoyable about shopping when you were a people-pleasing teenager who wanted to fit in.

You know the stress of 'back-to-school'? That pre-September nightmare where you buzz around like a dying wasp trying to get everything on The List before classes return? I was like that – all year round for about twenty years. From having the right clothes to having the right type of popcorn in my lunchbox – it had to be Manhattan, not generic Dunnes or Tayto – I had to be just like you to be liked by you and it was exhausting. I was the girl who said yes to smoking and listening to Blink 182 because you were doing it. Deep down I wanted not to die of an asthma attack and I wanted not to die while listening to Céline Dion. I didn't know who I was because I was a mirror. I just reflected what I saw around me. I was the plain rice base that gets flavoured by what it's paired with. I was the plain white wall that provides the perfect inoffensive background to whatever accented décor you choose.

At around fifteen I was questioning everything about myself. It seemed like I'd missed a developmental phase and all my friends knew who they were while I was still waiting to be handed a cast list with my role explained for me. We need a sense of self to feel alive, to feel worthy, and in the absence of my own identity, I looked to my friends. 'I know who Maria is, so I'll just be like her,' and the best way to do that was to say yes to everything she suggested.

The thing I didn't understand was that Maria was also trying to find herself. From the outside I thought all my friends knew what they were doing. I still feel like this sometimes. It's easy in the era of Instagram and social media to feel like everyone else has their shit together and I'm just flitting around like that dying wasp, trying to keep up. I look at videos of people lifting weights at the gym and think, How do they know how to do it properly? I look at people who have invested in stocks and shares and hear them talking about the economic implications of Brexit and think, How the hell do they know what to invest in? I look at people taking perfect casseroles out of the oven and think, Why does mine always look like something that's been regurgitated by a hippo? I hear people talking about pensions and putting their children in the right schools and feel like I've missed an instruction manual on how to be an adult.

It seems I've always felt that other people know something I don't. But they don't. They never have. Maria or Jane or Sally didn't know who they were when they went to Cork City to buy new shoes or a jumper. They were just teenagers too. Some were blindly following other trends and a few were braver, the leaders, the anarchists and trendsetters who decided they liked Buffalo boots and then we all followed suit.

Those teenagers who set the trends are a breed I still don't understand. It takes a level of confidence and fortitude to be the first person to stand up. They don't seem to be concerned about whether people stand up after them, or if they will be followed. Some are driven by their own desires, priorities and tastes and have little concern for who is watching. Ironically this makes them magnetic. A casual disregard for other people's opinion is very attractive.

I have no idea what separates one type of person from another. It could be nature, nurture or nonsense. Lots of people claim they don't care what other people think. Most of the time, I'm sure, that's a lie. I've said it in the past and it has certainly not been true. Since I was a teenager, I've spent the majority of my life trying not to care. I tell myself, sometimes on an hourly basis, even now, 'What other people think of me is none of my business.' It's easier at thirty than it was at sixteen. Back then, what other people thought of me was my occupation. It was a full-time job. And the job description was getting longer every day.

I had a daily to-do list that got longer by the second:

To Do

1. Be a good friend.

2. Be nice to everyone.

3. Share.

4. Be a good listener.

5. Be loyal.

6. Don't let people down.

7. Don't make a fuss.

8. Don't cause a scene.

9. Be a team player.

10. Say yes to everything.

11. Appear cool.

12. Watch MTV.

13. Be aloof and adaptable.

14. Never make the first suggestion.

15. Go with what the group wants.

16. Learn the lyrics to 'Stan' by Eminem.

All my friends had these little lists hidden beneath their hairbands and bobby pins. In our brains us girls kept a daily inventory of how good we were, where we came in the pecking order, who was annoyed with whom, which girls were popular, who was at the bottom of the bell curve, whose tastes had to be adopted, where the best seat in assembly was, who you needed to compliment and who needed to be shunned that day. Between that and managing our now raging hormones, adolescence was exhausting.

I wondered if across the road the boys in the boys' school were doing the same mental arithmetic to play by the unspoken rules as we were. They used to pass our school on their way to the sports pitches. They were always jumping on top of each other, kicking each other and running away, giving each other dead arms with one solid punch or just plain attacking each other. It seemed like being friends as boys was more demanding physically but a lot less effort emotionally. They were like little Neanderthals walking by our windows. They seemed uncomplicated and genuinely carefree as they marched towards the green in their little shorts carrying sticks to play hurling with. It felt like the only scores they needed to keep were on massive billboards over the pitch in plain black and white for everyone to see.

I was so busy with my to-do list, trying to get things right and fit in, that I wasn't able to figure out who I was or what I actually liked or disliked. I was such a hazy mix of everyone I was hanging out with that I needed my mother to make me feel vivid and clear and real. Because I couldn't do it for myself. Talk about an impossible task for a parent. I was coming home as a different person each day. It was like an amateur production of *The Importance of Being Earnest* where there are only two actors playing all the roles, and you get a migraine trying to follow the plot because each character is distinguished only by a different hat. I couldn't keep up with my ever-changing preferences and opinions, but I expected my mother to. Duh! That's why parents are for. 'You should have thought about having a teenager before you had a baby!' DOOR SLAM.

There's a long list of things I wish I'd said no to in secondary school. But I didn't know how. That was until Valeria arrived, but by then it was too late. Until Valeria arrived, I thought I was the only girl in the school who was constantly doing things she didn't want to do. I felt I was dying of chronic uniqueness, that no one could possibly understand the Stefanie Preissner plight. I thought all my friends were gifted with agency and autonomy and were uncompromising, self-actualised superheroes. That summer I learned that while I thought they all knew who they were I was wrong. All my friends were in the same boat as me. They all felt the creeping pressure of fitting in. We were like a load of hormonal lobsters getting slowly boiled in a pot of submission, surrender and sacrifice. After we met Valeria, we finally had a script, a template for what it is like to be ourselves. Valeria was the lobster who climbed out of the pot and scarpered, showing us that escape was possible. We watched while the water boiled around us.

One of my friends had Spanish students stay in her house every summer. That year Valeria arrived from Madrid and wanted to hang out with us more than with the other Spanish students and that was a big change. I bet she went on to great things. She was a genius, with perfect English, I assume perfect Spanish, and the Mediterranean complexion that Irish people can only dream of. Industries are based on everyone wanting to look like Valeria.

There was something about Valeria that took us fourteen-year-olds a while to work out. When we did, it was as baffling as it was eye-opening. No one ever, no Spaniard or Irish person, not a teacher, host, or taxi driver, had a bad word to say about her. That was a rare thing in a world that loves to moan and, particularly, a group of hormonal girls. She was beautiful, polite, intelligent *and* lovely. And no one resented her for it.

I stood back from the group and watched Valeria in action. I wanted what she had so I tried to use a scientific approach. I'd gather the data and analyse what she was doing. One conversation I remember went like this.

We were all sitting on the green, bikes and footballs, scooters and Nerf guns scattered around us, the detritus of childhood being lived out in the estate. Emma was using Brian's frisbee as a plate. Someone's parents had had a party which meant massive bags of pretzels and nuts were open for sharing. Loaded with sodium and parched, our eyes were darting around looking for water, until we realised no one had brought any so we'd just dig in for more crisps. Then, out of her tiny inflatable backpack, Valeria pulled a half-full bottle of water. She had a sip and popped it back in her bag. Emma was like one of the raptors in *Jurassic Park*. She scrambled onto her knees and tapped Valeria on her tanned, braceleted arm. (Where did those Spanish students always get those cool wristbands? I always wanted one and never found them.)

'Can I have a sip of your water?'

Valeria smiled. She whipped out an orange and a *box* of Spanish strawberry bubble gum. 'Would you like some of my orange? You have to try this bubble gum.'

Emma, obviously choosing to eat something sweet and juicy rather than drink plain old water, dived over me to hug Valeria. 'You think of everything!'

We ate the orange between us and it quenched our thirst. We talked about how sweet it was, as if we were citrus sommeliers.

Valeria was clearly an evolutionary stage ahead of us. She had worked out that if you say no to people it leaves a bad taste in their mouth. They are less primed to like you inherently. But she had boundaries and comfort zones. Valeria didn't want someone drinking from her bottle. Fair. So instead of saying no, she gave another option. I've seen people do it since and I always make a note to do it myself but I rarely remember. I often see it in restaurants.

'Can I have a Diet Coke, please?'

'We have Diet Pepsi?'

'Great, I'll have that.'

Now, cola-preference debates aside, it's sort of genius that the waiter never has to refuse the customer. They never have to say no. I'm sure there's some science behind humans hearing 'No' and feeling sullen about it so the counter-offer works. But when we were fourteen, Valeria had it down. She was beloved and beautiful and didn't have to drink backwash in her water.

Things I said yes to that Valeria would have counter-offered:

Smoking

'Do you want to try my cigarette?'

What Valeria would have said: 'Can I try your new Vans? I'm thinking of getting a pair.'

I ended up starting a habit that would be a monkey on my back for the next twelve years. Giving up smoking was the hardest thing I've ever done. And I've done a lot of difficult things. I imagine Valeria at the top of some very serene mountain, inhaling Alpine air through bronchioles that have never met a toxin in their perfect, stress-free lives.

Kissing Conor Bennett

'Conor wants to meet you behind the youth centre.'

What Valeria would have said: 'Will you ask him to meet me at the computers and play GTA with me?'

I went behind the youth centre because if I said no, the girls would think I was so uncool and the boys would think I was 'frigid'. That was the word they used, which became the barrier to saying no. 'You'd better do this or we'll tell people you're frigid.' I still don't know what frigid means. I imagine Valeria saving herself until the most perfect, respectful and charming Adonis approached her timidly, as you would an extremely rare and delicate bird. She's probably still with him today.

THAT haircut

'I'm going to chop into the back and go shorter with the layers, OK?'

What Valeria would have said: 'Could you leave the length and work your magic with my fringe?'

I spent 2002 growing out the worst haircut that has ever existed. There is a special place in hell for hairdressers who go against your wishes. It's still a massive weak spot for me. For some reason I find it impossible to say no to hairdressers. It's a vulnerable position they put you in. You're in their space, with a wet head and no make-up and they're all beautified and holding something really sharp close to your ear. I always feel if I go against what they're suggesting they'll roll their eyes, which they often do, and I'll feel so judged and ugly. It's like they're saying. 'Oh, you want me to do *that* to you, LOL, *okaaay*, but don't come crying to me when your awful taste in haircuts makes you a laughing stock. You're no Jennifer Aniston, love. I'll do my best with what I've got but . . . I've had better canvases, like.' I've travelled to Cork to get my hair done by Siobhan in Darcy's. I've made a return journey of five hundred kilometres to save myself the discomfort of saying no to hairdressers. Valeria's hair was kissed by Greek goddesses. I imagine the hairdressers who encounter it bow down to her and obey her command on each individual strand.

Teasing Sophie

'We should all start laughing for no reason when Sophie passes.'

What Valeria would have said: 'How about we leave Sophie to walk by unharassed and instead, Emma, you can enlighten us with another retelling about your trip to America?'

Peer pressure is bad enough when it puts you in an uncomfortable situation but I think peer pressure is the worst when it makes you force other people into discomfort. We bullied Sophie. There is no other way of saying it. The rules came down from on high and we all said yes because we were so terrified that if we said no we'd be the next Sophie. Kids are cruel and girls are the cruellest. I should have been stronger than that. In all of my people-pleasing, yes-saying life on this earth, in all the million minor yeses of my teenage years, the ones where I was too weak to say no, even when I knew it was the right thing to do, really stand out. I sometimes see old photographs of myself in a terrible hairstyle, or wearing clothing I was uncomfortable in, even hanging out with girls I now have nothing in common with, and I laugh or shrug or get a bit mortified for my young self. But there are also yeses I look back on with genuine regret. Bullying Sophie is one.

Kate, the alpha girl, had decided she didn't like her. We were all secretly terrified of Kate. She was the kind of girl who could change the temperature in the room with the raising of her eyebrow. I've even changed her name because, fifteen years later, I'm still a little afraid of her. She was like the villain in a Reese Witherspoon movie. Her disapproval was a social apocalypse you had to survive on your own. If you were in her good books, in her inner circle, her attention was like the heat of the sun. It warmed you, made you glow. But on the other side of that heat was a winter that not even a huddle of four thousand penguins could protect you from.

I don't know why Kate turned on Sophie but she did. She told us that we were to ignore her at all costs. If she spoke we were to pretend silence had filled the room. If she walked towards us we were to pretend she was invisible and keep walking. If she asked us anything we were to walk away. It was cruel and scary and disgusting. But we did it. For three full days we isolated Sophie out of the sheer fear of calling Kate out on her cruelty.

Eventually someone braver than I was threw a geography book right into Kate's face and told her she was a bitch. It took one girl to break the illusion of power and control Kate had over all of us. Sophie and the geography-book girl forgave all of us in Kate's harem for our behaviour. I would have understood if they hadn't. Sophie and I are friends today and sometimes I still apologise for what we did to her. She's over it. She says she was over it pretty much immediately but I'm not.

I've got better at saying no. I have on a few occasions as an adult – put a stop to that sort of mob mentality. I take Valeria's lead on this one. A subtle change of subject, or a diversion of some sort, works way better than outing the bully. I imagine Valeria mitigating the situation smoothly, and then she, Sophie and all the other teenagers get their nails done together and live happily ever after.

Buying labelled clothes

'It's only cool if it's got a tick emblazoned on it.'

What Valeria would have said: 'I really wanted to wear something pink. Can you help me find something?'

I only wore branded clothing as a teenager. One friend in our group set up her first email address and it was something like ilovenike@eircom.net.

I wish I could have said no to that kind of pointless peer pressure. I didn't develop my own taste in clothing until I was about twenty-eight. Even now I don't feel comfortable going out in anything even vaguely attention-drawing until I get the OK from The Boy Housemate. If I come downstairs in something new and his eyes flicker or widen even a millimetre, I'll go back upstairs and never wear it again. It's not a direct no, but I wish I could be comfortable enough within myself not to say yes to the endless trends, styles and taboos that surround what people are allowed to wear and when. *Let them wear Crocs*, I say.

Valeria has a distinct advantage here because Spanish students were always minimalist trendsetters when they came to Ireland. We can't compare wardrobes because we live in different climates. All I will say is that once Valeria and Co. had vamonosed back to Spain, Mallow saw a surge in the sale of inflatable backpacks. We did a little guffaw when she arrived with hers but we were all blowing into different shades of the same thing once she was gone.

There are several other things I wish I'd said no to as a teenager. Some of them – like that *terrible* haircut – were passing traumas but others have had a bigger effect. What the *hell* was I *thinking* plucking my eyebrows into two teeny tiny lines that went horizontally across my forehead? They looked like two emaciated caterpillars chasing each other from ear to ear. I wish I hadn't shaved above my knee. Now it's something I basically have to schedule – it's a time thief I could have spared myself if only I'd known. I also regret not saying no to Buffalo boots. I came off those whopper heels while descending the stairs of a Chinese restaurant and even now, years later, I still feel that niggle in my ankle when it rains.

I wish I could tell young Stef to say no to that coloured hair wrap-braid thing she insisted on getting in Mallorca. I ended up having to cut it out and still have a weird baby-hair section on my hairline where it never grew back properly.

I could also have done without uploading some terrifyingly

candid photos to Bebo. They still come up on Google searches and Bebo doesn't exist so I can't delete them. *Please don't go looking for them, I beg you.* I wish I'd said no to the garish MAC eye-shadows I insisted on buying and wearing. I looked like a mix between a drag queen and a Mexican sugar skull in some of those photos.

Do we all regret the first email address we set up? Why did no one tell us that putting 69 in your email address would probably hinder job applications? I wish I had said no when my friend convinced me not to do piano lessons because it clashed with SMTV live. I wish I'd said no to all those fizzy drinks that mean my head is full of mercury fillings right now. And I wish I'd said no to the impulse to choose a new polyphonic ringtone every time I was on public transport. I apologise if I've ever ruined a journey for you.

6

GRADUATION BALL. SOME PEOPLE CALL IT A 'PROM', others call it a 'debs' or 'the grads'. I call it the worst event of my life, ever. When you're seventeen, and even when you're an adult, 'no' is scary and hard. Saying yes means staying in the middle of the tribe and being safe. The sheep in the middle of the flock never get picked off by the foxes or wolves. It's the uncertain sheep, the ones who keep a little bit away from the flock or teeter on the edges in doubt, that are the first to go and the last to be missed. I bought my tickets for the debs without question because I didn't want to be remembered as

STEFANIE PREISSNER

DIED IN A MOMENT OF UNCERTAINTY IN 2005

PICKED OFF BY A WOLF AS SHE CUNSIDERED HER OPTIONS

RIP

I felt that if I had said no, to my graduation ball or to university, it would have been a defining no. I would become The Girl Who Said No.

The 'debs', as I called it, was a crucial part of my journey to becoming a yes-woman. If I view my journey as a climb up a treacherous mountain, the debs was the last possible refuge before I was on my own. There were warning signs I didn't see, massive placards that said, 'TURN BACK NOW: IF YOU PROCEED YOU WILL BE EATEN BY A BEAR.' (An Irish mountain would probably have a sign reading, 'DON'T COME CRYING TO US WHEN YOU'RE DEAD' or 'YOU'VE BEEN WARNED.' I continued to the summit without any thermals, no sherpa, no walkie-talkie, not even a flask of soup, utterly blind to the dangers ahead of me. Maybe the fake eyelashes were obscuring my vision. If I had turned back sooner I would have been spared the inclement weather and frostbite. By proceeding to the graduation ball, I continued along the road of 'going with the flow', 'people-pleasing' and doing things 'just because' everyone else was doing them.

At seventeen, the notion of all of my friends hanging out without me, of missing the Defining Night of our late teens, was unthinkable. A 'yes' from me made me normal, the same, unremarkable. We all scaled the mountain together. A 'no' would have put me in a little box with labels stuck to it. Defining labels, like 'shy', 'anti-social', 'boring', 'no fun', 'party-pooper', 'dry shite'.

The big yes, going to the debs, led to a series of smaller ones, all of which I wish I had said no to.

Here's how it went.

You *have* to get a new dress. And it *has* to be original. If anyone has ever laid eyes on your dress on anyone else *ever*, you fail at life. Now, I was an obese teenager so I was at least spared the risk of buying a high-street dress and showing up as someone's terrible twin. Instead, my mother had to fork out hundreds of euro to get a dress made for me. I looked like a large Chinese emperor. It was no fault of the dressmaker: she gave me exactly what I asked for. I'm not a designer and have a very poor taste in fashion: the material I chose was almost certainly intended to hang on rails in front living-room windows.

Next: you *have* to have a date and he has to be cool. Your family will quiz you about him for ever and your friends will judge you based on whom you choose so it can't be your friend's brother. I asked my closest friend at the time. Call him Donal. We had been friends since we were five. I wasn't concerned about the date part because Donal was a solid option. He agreed. Two weeks before the ball, Sandra asked him to go with her and he dumped me. We are no longer friends. I gave him several more chances after that offence. I shouldn't have. But each time he hurt me, the rules rang in my ears:

→ Be a good friend.

→ Be nice to everyone.

→ Share.

→ Be a good listener.

→ Be loyal.

→ Don't let people down.

→ Be a team player.

I should have said no to that friendship years before I did. But that's history now.

A true friend came to my rescue. Tom is a forever friend. He is endlessly kind, thoughtful and dependable. He didn't make a big issue of the fact that I hadn't asked him in the first instance. He stepped up, did his tie in a Cambridge knot, bought me a corsage and assured me we would have a great night. Tom and I survived our teenage years together by rolling our eyes at the crowd before we went along with them. We knew we had to play along to survive but we both knew we hated every minute of it. Tom's dad drove us to the hotel on the night of the debs. As we left the car we looked at each other.

'You ready?'

'No!'

'Me neither. But fuck it.'

'We're making memories.'

It was one disaster after another. Shane, the jock, was drunk by the time he got to the hotel. He'd been drinking on the bus on the way. Even now, in his early thirties, Shane can barely handle three pints so you can imagine the state of him in his dad's shoes stumbling towards the photographer, like something out of an apocalypse film. Drool and all. Understandably, his date Jenny was raging and upset and had to make sure everyone else would share the burden of her bad decision to bring Shane to the ball. She was crying into her corsage while Eva rubbed her back. Eva's date, a real Colin Firth type, tried to level with the bouncer who was trying to kick Shane out. Firth ended up getting barred, too, so now there were two snot streams running out of the blubber-huns in the corner. Eva broke up with the dashing Firth by text as the canapés arrived, and beelined for the cocktail sausages before high-tailing it to the bar to get sloshed.

Victoria and Emily had a fight because they were wearing the same dress. Emily claimed she was wearing a size 14 because Victoria had bought the last 12. 'AND I'M THINNER THAN YOU SO YOU DID IT JUST TO BE A BITCH.' A fake Louboutin flew across the dance floor.

There were very few actual couples at the debs. Most girls had brought someone they had their eye on, in the hope that they would blossom into a couple after that magical night. I think that came to pass for two couples. For everyone else, other people's dates were fair game. There is no honour among girls who think this is their last chance to kiss Barry Delaney. And they had no qualms about flirting with him in front of his date, Michelle. If Michelle had had the audacity to ask him out first, knowing he was too polite to say no, they had the audacity to seduce him in front of her. Barry Delaney was not to be seduced. By anyone. I have since clicked 'like' on his wedding photos to his husband Joseph and thus all mysteries from that night are solved.

The main course was listed as Turkey and Ham. In the midst of all the sloppy kissing and slobbery drukenness around me, the dryness of the meats was refreshing. It was a symmetrical delight having potatoes served to me with an ice-cream baller and I had forgotten since childhood my love of puréed root vegetables. A solid two stars. So far this had totally been worth the seventy-euro ticket. I wish there was a sarcasm font.

The dessert claimed to contain apple but it was too smothered in tinned custard and canned cream for the fruit to be detected. I ate it all the same. I also ate Tom's portion. By this time the music had kicked in and the dance floor was starting to heave. This gave me the opportunity to do what I did best: observe and judge while eating other people's desserts.

The boys had discarded their ties within fifteen minutes of scoffing their meal. Thirty seconds after the ties came off, the dance floor looked like an episode of *Takeshi's Castle*. Small men scattered on the floor, wriggling, writhing, climbing on each other's back and shoulders, pretending to be on rodeo bulls, or at the bow of the *Titanic*. It was carnage. No one knew whose date was whose. They all seemed to be wearing the same rented tuxedos, and without the ties there was no distinguishing them from each other. Unless you had intimate knowledge of how their sweat was distributed and how it might form an identifying pattern on their clothing, you had no hope.

I was gone the minute I heard someone suggest moving on to the Leisureplex. Sherpa or no sherpa I was turning around. Edmund Hillary can have the accolade, I'm going home. I called my mam to collect me and my date. He was probably keen to don some bowling shoes and re-enact the 'PinPals' episode of *The Simpsons* but he came home in the car with us. Maybe he, too, is a people-pleaser or perhaps simply horrified by what he had just witnessed. The car journey was made less awkward by his sunny retelling of the evening's events. I stayed quiet the whole way to Mallow. It was part-trauma and part-resentment of extrovert, people-pleasing Stefanie, squished into her Spanx on the car journey home.

I went straight up to my room. The figure-forming underwear came off me like the skin off a sausage. Mam had put a hot-water bottle in my bed. I crawled in and fell asleep, dreaming of what it might be like to enjoy bowling.

I now know that if I had said no to going to the debs there would probably have been girls who followed my lead and breathed a sigh of relief. A nice sea-level sigh where the oxygen levels are calming and you don't feel dizzy.

7

'THERE'S NO VIABLE CAREER IN THE ARTS. DROP MUSIC and art and do biology.'

'How about I do music and lay the foundations for the career I'm going to have, which is going to orbit the arts in some fashion? I think having a knowledge of and language for discussing music and entertainment will probably be of more use to me than knowing a mitochondrion is the powerhouse of the cell.'

OK, so no fifteen-year-old is ever going to speak to a career-guidance teacher like that.

Nor is a teenager likely to have Promethean foresight into what school subjects are going to be most applicable to them in the future. But, still, I should have said no to quitting music. Big regret. I imagine Valeria could have suggested, deflected and persuaded her way into Harvard. She never had to say no, but neither did she have to do anything she didn't want to do.

Saying yes to the CAO changed the course of my life. It's impossible for me to say what would have happened if I'd said no, but I didn't. I joined the corral of students who pile into the filter system to get into university. I didn't think there was another way to bridge the gap between school and career without going to university. But there is another way, and university isn't for everyone.

The Irish economy was booming in 2004-5, which meant that I, and many of my friends, would have been seen as crazy to say no to university. It was affordable to my family and most of my friends' families: it was just what people did. Going to university after your Leaving Cert was the next step. There were no other options – it was like washing your hands after using the toilet: if you didn't do it you were some kind of poorly raised degenerate. Even though you might not have known what you wanted to study, the prevailing attitude among our parents and teachers was 'Just go, pick any degree. You can switch once you're in there.'

In 2005, we wrote Irish essays about *an Tiogar Ceilteach* – the Celtic Tiger. In our tiger economy, degrees were free, people had loads of disposable income and, if they didn't, bankers were handing out free loans to anyone who asked.

Some are now in prison for their leniency when it came to financial regulation, while the people who accepted the loans are in figurative prisons, locked behind bars of debt with little chance of parole any time soon. In my world, not going to university had become a taboo. Not saying yes to the expectation of third-level education was a dangerous signifier to the adults in my life. They say that if children are cruel to animals it's an alarm bell: kicking a cat can be seen as an early warning sign of future delinquency, violence and criminal behaviour. When I finished school, saying no to university would have been seen as a similar indication of a dark future. If I'd walked away from the train of expectations, if I'd said no, it would have been seen – perhaps by me, too – as a first step on the downwards slope towards vagrancy. Once the summit of the debs was climbed, my journey to becoming a yes woman was much faster, much more linear and like most train journeys, filled with over-priced coffee.

I took my ticket and boarded the train of expectation. The first stop was university. Sitting on the plush seats, looking along the line to my future I could see the other stops on the route: university, then permanent and pensionable job, stable relationship, marriage, pension, mortgage and, inevitably, children were the towns and villages scattered along the tracks. At the very end I could see the last stop: Catholic funeral ceremony, the mourners reserved and elegant in their grief, and a headstone that reduced my existence to a name, two dates and one vague statement.

I did what I always do on trains. I drowned my thoughts in terrible music and distracted myself with expensive snacks.

I said yes to university because I felt it was the thing to do. I genuinely didn't question it. I wanted to be normal and do what everyone else was doing. There was no strong impulse or urge in me to do something different. Maybe my career-guidance teacher, or someone, should have explained that there were more than two options after Leaving Cert. University or a trade apprenticeship seemed to be the two streams. Taking a year off was for 'other people'. Travelling was for rich kids, usually with exotic accents, like Australians or Scots, maybe a Londoner or some American with a popped Ralph Lauren Polo shirt collar. Taking a year off was seen as wasting valuable time or irresponsibly losing momentum, and getting a full-time job was seen as too much pressure, too 'serious' for my years. So off I went.

Why?

Just because everyone was doing it. Going to college is the next step on the banal ladder of 'this is what we do now'. It's the next step in the dance routine.

Other such things include:

1. Sending Christmas cards to people you never see just because they're 'on your list'.

2. Obeying a dry-clean-only instruction.

3. Keeping receipts for ten years after all the ink has faded and they're illegible.

4. Not wearing white to a wedding.

5. Wearing black to a funeral.

6. Getting your car serviced every year.

7. Keeping your CV up to date.

8. Never texting a boy back straight away when he texts you.

9. Having a favourite book/film.

10. Tidying the house before the cleaner comes.

11. Saying ouch when you bump into something even if it didn't hurt.

12. Turning the radio down when you're lost while driving.

13. Running across the road if someone stops their car to let you cross just in case they think you're taking advantage.

14. Kissing people under mistletoe.

15. Being awake at midnight on 31st December.

16. Watching something scary on 31st October.

17. Wearing red/green to Christmas events.

18. Accepting the terms and conditions of something each and every time without reading them.

19. Hitting the enter and space bar key harder than any of the others on a keyboard.

20. Trusting people wearing hi-visibility jackets or hard hats.

21. Trusting the directions given by strangers.

22. Giving people a high-five when they offer one.

23. Needing your socks to match.

24. Rabbit being an OK food to eat but not cat.

5, 6, 7, 8. And turn, and kick, and heel, and toe,
Off to college now we go.
And job, and work, and car, and keys,
Then partner, house and families . . .

That's the 'Macarena' for middle-aged people.

It was the same pressure that people in their mid-to-late twenties feel when people keep harping on at them to GET ON THE PROPERTY LADDER. Getting through the gates of a national university was vital and time-sensitive. The early bird catches the worm, they say. But no one ever thinks about the worm: how did it work out for him being up that early, huh?

I wanted to study drama and theatre, so I said yes to university: if I had to study something it might as well be something I liked. My career-guidance teacher told me I would be better suited to primary-school teaching because it was very difficult to have a career in the arts. In response to my expression of interest in being an actor, she looked at me, head to toe, and said, 'You have to be incredibly striking or incredibly talented,' and handed me the teacher-training prospectus for Mary Immaculate College.

I guess I understand why school tries to encourage young people to be realistic in their career aspirations. I mean, if we all became what we wanted to be, the world would have an over-abundance of pilots, and NASA would be inundated. But there has to be a line. With every CAO application, or every essay we learn verbatim, a little bit of our youthful hope disappears. We become calcified into yes-people. Yes-people have 'realistic', 'workable' and 'secure' goals. I think we've all settled for less at some point. We regret not learning that musical instrument or dismissing our dreams of being professional athletes.

But, like, there *are* professional athletes. So why not you, right? The grossly unhappy, cynical bully you have for a boss would probably be the most vibrant, charismatic and enthusiastic colleague if he were in the career he wanted to be in . . . if he'd said yes to his instinct of what he enjoyed doing. I feel very fortunate that the course I chose in college – CK112 was the CAO code – set me up for the career I have now. Not everyone has had this experience.

Luckily, my mother encouraged me – well, 'encouraged' is a bit strong: she didn't forbid me, or try to turn me off the idea – of studying drama and theatre at third level. She insisted that I get a degree and advised that I take another subject to 'fall back on' if the drama didn't work out. I now have a whole vocabulary of Spanish and a detailed knowledge of *Don Quixote* which is of no use to me. But as Nana says, 'It's good for your CV.' If I had given in to the pressure put on me by my teachers to do something more 'sensible', I'd be a qualified primary-school teacher now. Every girl in my class who had a vibrant personality or a vivid imagination was directed towards teaching. I would be the worst primary-school teacher in the world. In my classroom, they wouldn't learn a single thing, except maybe some Disney songs. Luckily, I had enough adults in my life outside school to show me that a career in the arts was a valid option. They were the permission-givers.

What young people see shifts their perception of what is possible. For all of my childhood I believed that President of Ireland was a female role. I saw it as a job for a woman because it had always been held by a woman in my lifetime. It's the same with careers. If kids see diverse options, their minds open and those people become living versions of the word 'yes'. They give you permission to aspire to something. When I was in school, before I got into theatre, it seemed the only options were law, medicine, accounting or teaching. *Ally McBeal* and *Grey's Anatomy* definitely had a hand in solidifying this belief.

Maybe not becoming a primary-school teacher was the first big 'No' I ever said. I didn't look at it that way at the time. I was too busy running away from the idea of having to spend time with other people's children, wiping snot off little faces and putting on thirty pairs of gloves every snack- and lunchtime, to consider that I was saying a big 'No' for the first time. It didn't feel like a no, just as it doesn't feel like a no when I don't send money to the deposed King of Uganda's son whenever he emails me. However, if we're looking for a turning point in my journey to being a yes-woman, if we're putting my people-pleasing under a microscope to see where the cell divided and produced a negative response for the first time, you might say it was here.

It was a little win. It didn't feel like one because I shouldn't have gone to university at all, but I would have had to present a clear argument as to why it wasn't for me. Back then, that was beyond me. It's also pretty difficult to swim against the tide. I would have been like a tortured salmon swimming upstream, trying to dodge the swarms of trout and mackerel with their Clubs and Societies hoodies swimming against me.

What is it with people at universities and their need to tell you what their hobbies are through their choice of hoodies? I did it myself. I joined the UCC karate team just for the hoody. Didn't go to a single training session, but I wore the hoody every day. A big 'UCC' on the back and a man doing some sort of ridiculous and impossible karate chops! I wanted to be like all the other students while retaining my sense of humour. I chose the most ironic club hoody I could find. If I'd chosen rowing or frisbee or drama people might have thought I was really in the club and asked me questions or judged me based on my chosen sport. Anyone who saw nineteen-year-old Stefanie walking around the campus in her XXL karate hoody had no doubt she was being ironic: she was more about lamb chops than karate chops and you could tell.

There were obviously people in college who didn't wear club hoodies. I wondered about them. Even now I wonder about those who have a strong sense of style. I envy people who wake up in the morning, open their wardrobes, stand before them and think, What'll I wear today? At night I lay out my clothes for the following morning. It's always either dark blue or black jeans. If I'm being kind to myself or feeling unwell I allow myself to wear my 'good tracksuit' legs, with a black vest, some kind of unseen T-shirt and a black, grey, maybe red athleisure-style top. I have very little sense of what suits me or what I should wear. Smart-casual is the term I hear most when I ask people how I should dress. For me, there is nothing casual about clothing. And 'smart' is not a word that describes my approach to dressing. Nervous chic or pre-meditated anxious are more suited to my 'style'.

People who enjoy expressing themselves through their clothing are amazing. You have to have a strong sense of who you are and how you want to be seen to infuse your wardrobe with your sense of self. It's inspiring. I still don't know how to represent my personality in a colour, or with a neckline or a fabric, so I had absolutely no hope in 2005 when I started university. I saw people wearing hoodies and I thought, Great, I can just do that. Other people around me started experimenting with heels, coloured tights and unnecessary spectacles. I watched them play around with costumes until they found a look that matched the identity they were happy with. I kept the outline of a martial artist on my back hoping he would fight off any judgement, rejection or disapproval. For the most part, he did.

Well, maybe it was less him and more that, in the new environment, full of new people to convince that I was likeable, I redoubled my people-pleasing and yes-woman efforts.

8

MY EXPECTATIONS OF WHAT UNIVERSITY WOULD BE like were largely based on the fiction I had read and watched growing up. *Sabrina the Teenage Witch* and *Scream 2* were the main influences. The seasons of Sabrina attending Harvard were my least favourite and maybe that was what tainted my view of college. It seemed like all of my favourite shows became remarkably less interesting and relatable when the protagonists moved to third-level education. Zack Morris from *Saved by the Bell*, Tia and Tamera, even Cory and Topanga from *Boy Meets World* became boring simulacra of themselves after high school, so how was I to believe things would be different for me?

Scream 2 is my favourite movie in the Wes Craven franchise. It was the first thing I saw in which the university setting added to the excitement and plot. The sorority houses, the struggles to make new friends and the fact that the characters always carried books gave me what I considered a realistic idea of what college would be like: an education-focused, socially challenging but intellectually rewarding arena. It didn't set off alarm bells that I was forming my expectations on the back of a horror film.

University was horrific. Let there be no mistake. No, I didn't get hunted by a serial killer, watch my friends get butchered around me or labelled 'That's the girl whose mom got murdered' but it was still nightmarish.

During that time my people-pleasing tendencies reached their peak. Whatever chance I had of saying no to the people I'd gone to school with, I had none whatsoever of asserting myself with strangers I needed to be my friends, classmates, housemates. I couldn't allow myself healthy boundaries while I was developing a new network. Saying no to parties and mixers and club nights would have meant never meeting anyone outside a lecture hall: social suicide. So I muted Little Stef, the still small voice inside me who just wanted to be at home in her PJs, watching TV or reading or playing a board game with friends. If you want to play board games with friends you have to make some friends.

On Clubs and Societies Day, I struggled to say no to the people who were handing me biros and clipboards in an attempt to get me to sign up to stuff I didn't want to do. To this day I get emails from the Stitch 'n' Bitch society who meet on a Monday to knit and sew while venting their woolly spleen about the upset *du jour*. I was so hell bent on saying yes that I joined Young Fianna Fáil, Young Fine Gael and the Young Labour Party. When I told my grandfather, he said that no granddaughter of his would vote anything other than Fianna Fáil. Since then I've had a heartfelt respect for the privacy of ballot boxes.

University is a particularly difficult time for people-pleasers. I wanted to start saying no and drawing fresh boundaries because these were new people who knew nothing about me. In college, you have *carte blanche* to redefine yourself, but because everyone is deciding who they want to be, it becomes even harder to say no – if you do, whatever you've turned down becomes a defining feature of your personality. If you miss that first foam party, you're the girl who doesn't do foam parties. Again, most of my experience with such labels relates to some Hollywood fiction or other. In particular, I avoided:

1. The girl who doesn't have time for fun.

2. The girl who doesn't smile.

3. The girl who can't say no.

4. The girl who does the work.

5. The girl who doesn't have sex.

1. The girl who doesn't have time for fun

I learned this one from Sabrina the Teenage Witch when she went to university. Sabrina struggles to juggle her hectic university schedule and all the social demands made on her. She is working 'double time', which means stealing time from her new friends Roxy and Miles, who move incredibly slowly. This trope pops up over and over again in popular culture and in real life. The girl who doesn't have time is dripping with extracurriculars. In UCC I knew one: she was the president of three societies, had a different hoody for every day and was also a genius in her commerce class. She was always in the library because sacrificing her education at the altar of her hobbies was not an option. No one wanted to hang out with her – not that she'd have had time – because, subconsciously, we felt like wasters and underachievers around her. She never got invited to anything because we assumed she wouldn't have time. Sabrina nearly lost her friends and her place in college because of her poor time management. I was adamant not to become that girl. Time for fun had to be worked (casually) into my schedule.

2. The girl who doesn't smile

I had been avoiding this label long before I went to university. I had managed until then to appear smiley enough, but now that I was in a new environment, where I was pretty uncomfortable most of the time, I had to make a big effort not to become the Girl Who Doesn't Smile. Early on in college I realised that another girl bore this tag so I could ease up a little. Surely, I thought, there isn't room for two.

The Girl Who Doesn't Smile was always in the library or floating around campus. She usually wore interesting clothes and was beautiful in an aggressive, stark kind of way. People noticed her and were attracted to her but she said no to the social necessity of greeting strangers. She'd meet my friendly smile in the coffee queue with a swift cold shoulder or, if we were walking, an abrupt change of direction. No one knew what she studied but everyone knew who she was. People mistook her seriousness for loneliness and, at the start, she was often invited to things. People pitied her. When she said no, which she always did, she became defined by her solemnity. Pity turned to contempt and she was left alone, whether she liked it or not.

3. The girl who can't say no

This was the definition I had to work hardest to avoid. It was the identity I was most likely to assume without any effort or intention, but television had taught me I would rue the day I became that girl. She's just too eager. She makes people nervous and uncomfortable with her free-floating enthusiasm. The girl who can't say no is so desperate to be included and invited that she repels people. I had seen enough of the Stephen King-style humiliations that happened to this girl to know she was one to avoid at all costs. The character that calcified the stereotype for me and made me adamant never to be that girl was Luna Lovegood in the Harry Potter books. In college, there was so much opportunity for me to become a Luna. Plans were always made late in the day, which unsettled me. I had to bite my tongue to refrain from asking people if they were going to this party or that night out.

4. The girl who does the work

Another persona I could have adopted all too easily. We've all seen *Friends*, right? From the very first episode Monica sets herself up as the mother of the group. She's the Girl Who Does the Work. In the pilot episode we learn how difficult this defining title is to shuffle off. Rachel bursts into the coffee house in a wedding dress, having a panic attack, to find Monica, *who she hasn't seen since college*, so that Monica can comfort her. Monica spends the episode tidying up Rachel's life, comforting Ross in his heartbreak, giving out to Joey, and parenting Phoebe and Chandler.

On my first night at university, everyone in the house played poker to loud music, then drinking games. The following morning the house looked like a crime scene. It took every ounce of discipline in my DNA to stop me cleaning it. I'd seen what happened to that girl. She can't say no to other people's disgusting habits. She can't say no to people eating her food, using her Tupperware and being generally closer to pigs than humans in shared living spaces. I knew I had it in me to offer a level of comfort to my housemates by cleaning up after them. I knew I'd probably get lots of social-media praise and shout-outs on Instagram if I cleaned up after that first party. But I also knew, from ten seasons of Monica being exploited, that there would be no way out for me. I stood in the chaos of the living room when another girl entered. She picked up six empty cans on her way to the kitchen area. She put the plug into the sink and sealed her fate. She became the girl who did the work.

I fell foul of the label myself in Spanish class when we had group research projects to do. I'd find myself up late at night googling Cervantes while the rest of my group were checked in to Redz nightclub on Facebook. It suited me because I enjoyed having an excuse not to go out, but I was still being taken advantage of. Even if it suits you to do the heavy lifting, it's still nicer if someone offers to help. This is probably the definition I had least success in avoiding, but if I had to be lumped with one of them, I was almost OK with being known as the girl others could depend on for an academic dig-out.

5. The girl who doesn't have sex

This came straight from the *Scream* movie franchise. Apparently it's a rule in horror movies that once a girl is no longer a virgin she can be killed. In the film, Randy's rules for surviving a horror movie were:

1. You may not survive the movie if you have sex.

2. You may not survive the movie if you drink or do drugs.

3. You may not survive the movie if you say 'I'll be right back', 'Hello?' or 'Who's there?'

Seeing university as a real-life horror movie, I struggled to try to find a balance between keeping those rules and not being defined as the Girl Who . . . doesn't do those things.

In *Scream 1*, Sidney gets attacked about twenty minutes after losing her virginity to her boyfriend, Billy, and that wasn't a risk I was willing to take. On the other hand I'd watched a lot of *Clueless*, and when Tai throws the line 'You're a virgin who can't drive' at Cher, I knew there was something deeply shameful about it. Cher is identified as a virgin early in the film and it's one of the more difficult tags to rid herself of.

In UCC I heard a girl described as frigid or 'a tease' because some douchebag had propositioned her before she'd even put the sheets on her bed on night one. With his ego bruised he'd go telling his male friends she was a prude and his female friends that she was a bitch. I was terrified. I went back to *Scream 2* and took my cue from the sorority girls who 'promoted safe sex'. I thought that seemed like the sensible thing to do. Being safe was a label I could cope with.

I was going against all of my natural instincts by avoiding cleaning up, not looking for definitive party schedules, trying to smile at strangers and not burying myself in my school work. Little Stef, the quiet voice inside me, was screaming. She was begging to be heard, to be listened to. She knew, long before I did, that I was playing with fire. If you ignore who you really are for long enough, you'll disappear. It's like hunger. If you ignore it for long enough, your body's signals stop. Eventually you collapse.

My collapse came in the form of an actual collapse. But I had more yeses to give before it got to that. I had stopped saying no for so long, I don't know if I still understood the word.

When 'Stephen with a ph' came along and asked me out I forgot that 'No' was even an option. I had forgotten I had a choice. He wanted to go out with me so that was what we did. It had been so long since I'd taken my desires into account that they'd sort of stopped existing.

In *Scream 1*, Sidney's boyfriend turns out to be a serial killer. When she goes to university, we were all on the edges of our cinema seats, Diet Coke beside us, fists full of popcorn, ready to be told her new boyfriend Derek is the new killer. Surely he must be. A man who openly declares his love for a woman he's known just a few months, publicly and *through song*, is surely some kind of psycho. So, I was cautious about Stephen because boyfriends are always the killers, university or no university.

Although he never serenaded me in the main restaurant at UCC, Stephen was a nice guy. He seemed to find me entertaining. He texted me often, looking to sync our free time so we could meet up. He liked the way I was passionate about the arts. He liked my perfume. He liked to drive to my house and hang out with my friends, and it didn't matter that the feeling wasn't mutual. I said yes to hundreds of cinema dates, I didn't say no when he ordered food for both of us, even though I would have chosen something different. I said yes to the countless lengthy phone calls for which I didn't have time or energy. I bore witness to the endless swiping through family photographs of beach holidays I had no interest in. I aged in real time with that boy and not for one minute did I believe I could say no. There was nothing torturous, malevolent or sinister about Stephen. He was a lovely respectable boy who wanted to be my boyfriend, and for me, that was all a relationship was. I was his girlfriend because he wanted me to be.

It had been so long since I took stock of what I wanted that I forgot I even had a choice. I just went along, as though I was in an inflatable swimming ring on a lazy river. I got carried along on the current of his choices. If I'd seen the white-water rapids ahead, I might have got off when I could still reach the riverbank. Like, if Sidney Prescott could have seen the murder and carnage ahead of her at the end of *Scream 2* maybe she would have opted not to go to university. And if the *Scream* sequel had opened with her choosing not to further her education, the killer would have shown up wherever she did decide to go.

You can't avoid the killers or the noes for ever. I may have been prioritising Stephen's wishes over my own, facilitating other people's social lives by doing their academic work for them, letting my housemate clean up so I didn't have to, and pretending to enjoy socialising, but at least I wasn't the Girl Who People Had a Concrete Reason Not to Like.

The yeses carried me all the way through my three years at college. Yes to the law ball, yes to lunch every Wednesday, yes to waiting around campus for three hours, bored out of my mind, just to see him for twenty minutes before his bus took him home for the weekend. Yes to parties with his friends. Yes to screenings of Marvel movies I hated. Yes to food I didn't like. Yes to babysitting his nephew. Yes to remembering the significant dates in the lives of his family and reminding him of them. Then yes to buying presents from him to his family members. Yes, yes, yes to a million little atrocities.

Eventually, saying yes freed me. I said yes to a weekend away with him in some European capital. He booked the cheapest Ryanair flight to some satellite town within 100 kilometres of the city. I said yes to every bad suggestion. Yes to a budget hotel. Yes to street-vendor food. Yes to watching an Ireland match in an Irish pub. Yes to singing rebel songs with strangers who'd become drunkenly patriotic and grotesque. Yes to being the sober one so we could safely find our hovel of a hotel.

Eventually, after I'd watched Stephen incapacitate himself with overpriced Guinness, my feelings became so strong I couldn't ignore them. What was I doing there? Who was this man? If he fell off his bar stool right now and cracked his head, would I care? No. It was the first no in our relationship. It was the start of the end. By the time our flight landed (ahead of schedule: cue the trumpets) at Dublin airport, Stephen and I were broken up. He hadn't paid the six extra euro to ensure we were sitting together. It was the best mistake he'd ever made. We walked down the shaky steps to disembark the aircraft, then walked side by side through security. Outside the airport, Stephen suggested getting separate taxis home. He was suggesting it for me to say, 'No.' I knew he wanted me to convince him we should travel together, that there was something to be salvaged and a forty-euro taxi ride would be the perfect time to do it. Clearly he hadn't taken note of how difficult I found it to say no. 'Yes,' I said, 'you're right.' And we made two Dublin cab drivers forty euro richer.

9

I JOINED MALLOW ACROBATICS CLUB AND MALLOW
Pyramid Gymnastics Club a total of thirteen times. The last
time I tried to sign up, I took Mam to the old school hall
where the classes were held. The smell of feet hung in the air
and condensation dripped down the walls. The head coach
took my mother aside and told her not to waste her money.
He knew from experience how this would go. My mother
would hand over her money and I would attend the club for
three weeks. In the first week I'd be the star pupil because
I'd done the forward-roll class twelve times already. The

following week we'd get onto backwards rolls and I'd be used as the demonstration, such was my perfect technique. But in the third week we'd get into trouble when the cartwheel required me to throw my head towards the ground and hope my hands would save me. Every time we got to the cartwheel I would quit. I'm thirty years into the journey of learning how to cartwheel and I still can't do it.

I'm just explaining to you that I don't always pick things up very quickly. You may have been thinking, Oh, great, we've got to the part where Stefanie's learned to say no, or Stefanie has turned a corner in the road and is now on a journey away from being a yes-woman. Maybe when I didn't become a primary-school teacher you thought that too. Well, if that was your thought, you can backflip right out of it. Saying no to my relationship with Stephen was just a red herring in the plot of my yes-woman story. Ditto with the teaching. It's the literary equivalent of the chief of police being given a feet-first introduction in *Scream 1*. In the movie we see the officer's boots before we see his face, and they're the exact same boots as the killer was wearing in the previous scene. The audience is tricked into thinking we've now been shown the killer and the movie will progress with the dramatic irony of the audience having more information that the protagonist. But it's not so. No no no. The chief of police is not the killer in *Scream 1* and I had many more hoops to jump through to round off my yes-woman career.

In June 2006, I was in university, focusing mainly on my drama and theatre studies degree but keeping up pace in the Spanish department. It takes two subjects to tango your way into an arts degree and although I had never studied Spanish before, languages come easy to me and I loved it. What I hadn't anticipated, however, was the Erasmus year you have to do when you study a foreign language at third level. Move abroad for a year? No, thank you. No way. Not happening. It wasn't simply that I didn't want to move to a foreign country, away from all my routines and supports, I also didn't want to leave the fifteen people in my drama and theatre studies class and have to come back and do my final year with the group below me. I numbed this particular anxiety with paella until I was brave enough to confront it.

University isn't as prescriptive an environment as school, but they do have some rules. Erasmus seemed like one of them. I spoke to the head of the Spanish department. I didn't say no. I had only just become aware of the no muscle: flexing it twice in one year was a big ask. Instead of putting my foot down, I begged, I pleaded. I expected the stern, polished response of a matador, but they told me that my grades were excellent and if I went to Spain for a month in the summer, worked extra hard in Third Year and wasn't concerned about joining the Third-Years who were arriving back from their year in Spain, I could proceed. *Arríba!*

I went back to my student accommodation and told a friend of mine the good news. She was more excited than you usually are for someone who has moderately good news. It didn't take long for her ulterior motive to come out. She had been chatting to another friend of ours, Emily, about going away for a month in the summer. They were thinking of interrailing or backpacking somewhere, but if I was moving to Spain for a month, they'd just go there. I raised my eyebrows – but not in the right way. I should've raised them in a questioning, semi-cautious way. But I didn't. I raised them in a pleasantly-surprised-you're-inviting-me kind of way. I should have said no at this point. But I didn't.

Three is a terrible number. It's just awful. There is always two plus one and the one is either a dictator, igniting feelings of resentment in the other two, or is excluded as the other two combine their motives to make democratic decisions go their way.

The Spanish you learn in UCC is Castilian. It's the Spanish that's spoken in most of Spain. It is distinctly different from Catalan, which is spoken in Catalunya. Barcelona is the capital of Catalunya and Catalans have fought hard to preserve Catalan as the spoken language. I had no business trying to improve Castilian Spanish in Barcelona, but two yeses overrule a no so we moved to Barcelona for four weeks. We booked an apartment a twenty-minute train ride outside the city. I liked being in student accommodation where we could self-cater, and we had a pool.

My compadres, in holiday mode, did not see this as I did – as an extension of my second year at university. They wanted to live closer to the city because the train stopped at 11 p.m. and started at 6 a.m.: if we wanted to go out, we were tied to timetables. That kinda suited me, and I think it annoyed the girls that I wasn't pushed. I was the only one who had Spanish so they needed me around and that shifted the balance of power in the wrong direction.

I've lost track of all the things I should have said no to

during that trip. Gillian knew me intimately from living with me in Cork. She knew I was unlikely to want to go out every night, if at all. Emily and I didn't know each other that well. If we had, we would probably have been able to salvage a friendship from that trip. My fear of crowds, loud noises, and being out of my comfort zone made her feel like she was spending her holiday in a too-regulated summer camp.

One night, about two weeks in, I wanted to stay in AGAIN and they wanted to go out. We had met some English boys in an Irish bar and they were going to Port Olímpic, a strip of clubs and bars on the marina. We had passed the place and even in daytime it looked too buzzy for me. Every suntanned cell in my body was screaming, *Please no*. But I felt this was almost a test. If I didn't say yes, all the noes I'd been saying for the past two weeks would erupt all over us.

We waited under stone arches for a thunderstorm to pass. It was 8 p.m. and we were meeting the boys for dinner first. We had a call from 'Rick from Scotland' with a last-minute change of plan. (You can imagine my delight.) They had some work to do at 'Alistair's place': would we come there, get pizza and go out later. It wasn't a question. It was an instruction phrased like a question. Emily agreed for us all. Alistair said he'd 'send a car'. So we got into a stranger's car, to drive to a stranger's house and get drunk cheaply before leaving with the strangers to get drunk more expensively.

At Alistair's, the ceilings were only marginally higher than some of the people scattered around the apartment. The opulence dripped off the penthouse walls, like the condensation on the side of the Moët bottles in the cooler.

Alistair welcomed us. He stood topless, in shorts and designer flip-flops, a heavy gold chain lying around his thick neck. His beer belly had enjoyed the sun for several months. At the back of his head, a roll of fat covered a line of skin that betrayed his skin tone when his head moved forward. I caught a glimpse of it when he did a mock-curtsy to welcome us, a champagne bottle in each fist.

Alistair was a thirty-four-year old Liverpudlian. He had five guys working for him in Barcelona. Our contact, Rick, was nineteen and had moved to Barcelona a month previously to work for him. 'What do you guys do?' was a question the three of us asked on a loop that night. Each time the answers became more imprecise and ranged from 'We sell things to grannies' to 'It's a delivery company.' I was too scared to push for the real answer. The apartment was so flashy, the gold chain and the champagne, there was no way this was above board. The first instalment of the night involved pizzas and kebabs delivered to the house. I sat next to them for safety. Alistair showed the other girls around. He had a pool, a drinks cabinet, two four-poster beds and a massive flat-screen TV with the BBC channels on it. I heard him say they could try the pool 'later'. Fuck.

For all his wealth, there was only one goddamn bathroom. I know this because every time I tried to go, one of the lads was in there. They would go in for thirty seconds and come out without flushing. I was too innocent to suspect drugs. There were as many noes for me to say as there were grains of cocaine on the fifty-euro note Alistair handed me to buy the first round of drinks when we eventually got to Port Olímpic.

The night performed its terrible dance.

At one point I went to the toilet and my worst fears came true. I came back and Gillian and Emily were gone. So were the guys.

I started calling Gillian. No answer, not that either of us could hear our phones over the multiple bass lines from the strip of clubs that all converged in my head.

I made my way to the main road, away from the strip. I was calling with my voice and with my phone and each was futile. A car horn beeped loudly and at length. Across the road the scene played out in front of me, like an episode of *Skins* meets *Trainspotting*. Nineteen-year-old Rick from Scotland had run out in front of a taxi. Emily was standing on the grass, on the other side of this terrible show, watching it in horror. The taxi driver beeped, presumably in shock at nearly knocking Rick down.

In response to being beeped at, Rick (whose jaw seemed to be rocking at the bottom of his skull from whatever drug he'd taken) kicked the wing mirror off the taxi. The taxi driver, and all the taxi drivers in the area, got out of their cars and started chasing Rick. Alistair saw this and summoned his men. One of the taxi drivers punched Rick in the face and was set upon by some of Alistair's guys. The scuffle was punctuated by Emily screaming, 'Stop, stop, stop!'

Rick got away and ran past me. Emily yelled at him to come back. All I heard was 'If we were in Glasgow', in his thick Scottish lilt, and an instruction from Rick to Alistair: 'Get me a knife.' At that point I was done. I wasn't waiting until 6 a.m. to get a train. I'd cut my losses and spend sixty euro on a taxi home.

The drivers didn't get back into their taxis quickly enough. I waited another thirty minutes by the side of the road. The dead heat lay on me like a heavy synthetic blanket. There was not enough air on that street for everyone present. The palm trees were unmoving above us, backlit by the glow from the neon lights lining the marina. At 4.30 a.m. I decided to go to twenty-four-hour McDonald's and eat Eurosaver Menu delights until it was time for the train.

When I got home, Gillian was asleep in bed. She's such a chirpy little drunk person – she has an endlessly sunny personality. The night's trauma hadn't reached her: when she'd got bored, she'd taken a taxi home and gone to sleep. I filled her in on the night's events over coffee, and she took it in as though I was telling her the plot of a film.

Emily had also gotten a taxi home and was asleep on the couch.

The following day I rang Mam and asked her to book me a flight home. I did a backwards roll out of the place over a week early. It was too much.

The Spanish department still think I was there for a month, not that it matters. The following summer, almost to the day, I passed my Spanish degree with second-class honours. And I haven't used it since.

10

I CAME OUT OF MY EDUCATION SO INSTITUTIONALISED
I couldn't put a value on myself. Without teachers around
to grade me, praise me, or tell me where I could improve, I
had no sense of how I was doing in the world. Was I adulting
properly? Was I correct? Was I doing the dance moves right?
I was so insecure and desperate for some kind of approval
and validation that I would have said yes to *any* job offered to
me. Graduates are often in this position. It's almost as if we're
meant to feel honoured to be added to the workforce, that we
should be grateful for any crumbs tossed at us from the table
of employment.

This feeling of desperation, need for validation and acceptance, which would eventually be coupled with the JobBridge scheme in Ireland, was nothing but a recipe for exploitation.

JobBridge was set up in Ireland in 2011 in response to the awful economic downturn that led us into a recession. It was a government initiative to help unemployed people to get work experience. It sounded like a genius plan – to edge people who had been claiming long-term jobseeker's benefit into work as interns for a company. The employee would get an extra fifty-two euro on top of their social welfare payment and the company got a free worker.

There were massive barriers to work: you needed experience to get a job but you needed a job to get experience. JobBridge was meant to bridge that gap. But that was not what happened. Many companies took in the free workers and had them working full-time with full responsibility but none of the perks, like wages or a pension. Yet people were queuing up for these internships. Why? Because of the need to feel useful, wanted and valuable in the field we'd trained in. The Boy Housemate tells me that one of the most defining jobs of the JobBridge era was as a 'sandwich artist' in a chain of cafés that sells only sandwiches. He gets quite riled up when he talks about it. 'They were just replacing full-time employment with these subsidised workers. It should have been a criminal act. No one wants to do an internship learning how to fill sandwiches and cut them. That's not an internship. That's exploitation.' He also says that I hadn't heard of the sandwich-artist internship because I've never had to look for work. That is not true. Maybe I've never had to look for that *kind* of service-industry, customer-facing, retail-ish work, but I *have* earned my place on the merry-go-round of frustration with precarious employment.

The Boy Housemate is correct: there was no JobBridge for actors but that didn't prevent me from saying yes to working for free, on anything, anywhere, day or night, rain or snow, fed or unfed. In theatre they call it 'profit share' because it sounds slightly better than 'unpaid'. We all know that the arts rarely make a profit so it's the elephant in the room we all choose to ignore.

If you got Scouts badges for doing profit-share shows, my sash would be covered. There'd be the skull patch from when I played four roles in a production of *Hamlet* in the basement of my friend's dad's shop. There'd be the aeroplane badge from when I was in an English translation of a French play called *11 September 2001*. I'd surely have been given a spaghetti-bowl badge for a production of a new play called *Casa Lisa* in which I played a fifty-year-old cook named Greta. A fishing badge would have been bestowed upon me for my contribution to a play whose title escapes me but in which I held a fishbowl for the entire show and poured the water steadily out of it until the fish died. I think it was meant to be some metaphor for mortality but I just had to explain to everyone who threatened to call PETA that it was a fake fish, which ruined the illusion and the point of the whole thing.

There's one badge that should have been a medal. They give army veterans medals to thank them and apologise for the atrocities they faced while serving, don't they? I should get one of those medals for a production of *The Comedy of Errors*, which I performed in Shakespeare in the Park in St Stephen's Green in the summer of 2010. I still don't know what that play is about. I know that we didn't have enough male actors – usual story in Irish theatre – so we did that gender-reversal thing where the women played men. We debased ourselves by handing out flyers in costume on Dublin's main shopping thoroughfare. Trying to get audiences to come to anything free is impossible: they just don't value the work. The show was a chaotic matrix of getting changed in small tents, trying to protect the tents from the homeless people who lived in the park, keeping the attention of Chinese tourists who didn't understand the plot, and making sure we kept up the collective illusion that we were enjoying the process.

I've heard people in the media say that young people are rude, entitled snowflakes, who have notions. We should be grateful for all of the zero-hours contracts being thrown at us, for the offers of internships where we can learn to lay pepperoni on pizza bases before or after cheese triangles, or eighty-hour weeks with too much responsibility. I'm fascinated by their point of view. They say we have too many options and blame Netflix for making us feel we're entitled to choice. It's bizarre because, from where I'm standing, there is a broken system in which the options are extremely scarce. You can't say no to unpaid exploitative work because you need experience to get a job and have to work for free to get experience.

When I was in school we were told that the world was our oyster. We had all the options in the world available to us.

That's the fallacy of choice. Once you do your graft to get the experience you need, it's fair and vital that you put a value on yourself and try never to go below it. But there will always be people trying to get a bargain. I know the feeling I get when I buy something at full price only to see it on sale in the shop down the road. I feel duped and foolish. This is the same feeling whether you're talking about a chocolate bar or an entire workforce. I understand not wanting to pay for something when other people are getting it for free. But this becomes problematic when the 'something' is people.

By and large, people want to work. I desperately wanted to work. I wanted to feel like the effort and the amount of time I had put into my education, my actor training, had been worth it. I needed to see a light at the end of the tunnel – the tunnel being all those days I'd spent learning the various imaginative uses of a large wooden cube in an improvisation (seat, table, footstool, rock, small child, television set, toilet, coffin, corpse, corpse *in* coffin, etc.). I'm sure if I had studied commerce, law or even physiotherapy, I would have been equally enthusiastic to put into practice what I had learned. It's this wide-eyed enthusiasm, and the pent-up practical application of our knowledge that makes graduates so easy to exploit.

I knew that making an idiot of myself for Shakespeare in the Park was not the life I wanted to live. I knew that something was wrong but I had no control. I had no agency. (And no agent at that point. With no hope of getting one if I kept doing those terrible shows.) I had spent so many years being compliant, obedient and accommodating that I had almost forgotten I even had a preference. Saying no was for other people, people who had fortitude and courage. My head was melted. But I hadn't hit rock bottom or seen the light yet.

I picked myself up, made a fuss in my head trying to work out how to change my life but eventually talked myself back onto another stage in another profit-share production. It was probably called *Much Ado About No Thing*. (It definitely wasn't called that. But I might yet write that play.)

11

AFTER COLLEGE, I WAS INTRODUCED TO A WOMAN WHO loves to give presents. Sounds like the perfect addition to anyone's army of comrades, no? Well . . . not so much. I wish this was a story from my childhood – then it might have been a little endearing. Unfortunately I was a fully fledged adult, at the top of the bell curve of my yes-woman career.

This woman, Heather, is quite powerful in the theatre industry. She either likes or hates you, and if she likes you, you feel the warmth of her affection so intensely you get a sun tan. She can turn on a whim, though. I have observed people approach her like Border Collies approach capricious owners; scanning their face intently, trying to read them. She's someone whose mood you need to work out before you engage or you could find yourself torn to bits. When I was working with her, about ten years ago, we had a group text message going – pre-WhatsApp: the first person to encounter Heather on a morning would inform the rest of us as to what her mood was like. We called it the Heather Forecast and it got us out of many a difficult day. You could disrupt a bad weather system by bringing her a perfect coffee order or make a sunny mood last a week by playing your cards right. It was a lesson in tip-toeing and people-pleasing. A class no one should have to take.

Heather liked me. I was so adept at people-pleasing by my twenties that I never upset her enough to disturb the cruel silt that rested beneath the surface. Everyone knew this, so I was often tasked with being the bearer of bad news, which I would always serve dressed in a good-news sandwich, with a steaming hot coffee, milk in first, two Canderel, in a pre-scalded ceramic mug with no 'slogans or platitudes' printed on it.

I had a big birthday early in the first year I knew Heather. Birthdays and Christmas were her time to make public how she was dividing her respect and admiration for her staff. One year she gave three people on her five-person team iPods while the other two got a selection of herbal teabags in a decorative jar. I didn't ask for the day off for my birthday. I knew that Heather wouldn't look kindly on an expression of self-interest. I decided I would come in early, be there when she arrived, my head buried in my laptop and my headphones on to indicate intense focus. I'd get tacit Brownie points for that.

That morning, Heather came in with a small Brown Thomas bag. The store's distinctive black, cream and gold bags immediately convey indulgence and luxury. She carried it on her baby finger and did a lap around the office, just to make sure the other girls (who had actually been in earlier than me) got a chance to see it. Then she came up behind me. Placed the bag in front of me, over my shoulder. Leaned in and kissed the air next to my ear. Although The Fray were singing to me through my headphones I caught the 'Happy birthday, sweetie' whisper before she catwalked to her desk. The Heather Forecast popped up on my Nokia.

What is it?

Careful it's not anthrax.

Wonder if she just keeps the Brown Thomas bags and re-uses them.

I took the bag into the kitchen while Heather was on a call. A few others gathered around me as I unwrapped a little box. I opened a small black pouch and emptied its contents into my hand. Two pearl earrings stared up at me, like confused eyeballs. They were objectively beautiful but they instigated one of those waves of muted laughter among us. Why were we laughing at the earrings? Because *my ears aren't pierced*. One of the girls was sent out on a coffee run soon afterwards and took a sidestep into Brown Thomas. She texted the group to tell us the earrings were worth €249. We wondered if maybe Heather had been given them and didn't want them. But her

PA confirmed from her bank statement that she had bought them the previous day.

I did some research on how to care for pearls and printed three copies of my findings. I left one where I knew Heather would 'happen' to see it that lunchtime. After lunch I knocked timidly on her door. Permission to enter granted, I took one step in, looked at Heather, shook my head and smiled. 'I'm sorry I didn't come to you sooner, I haven't really worked out what to say. Thank you so, so much, Heather. I can't believe I own pearl earrings. They're just gorgeous. I'll cherish them. I've already decided I'm wearing them to my cousin's wedding. And I promise I'll take the *best* care of them.'

'I'm so glad you love them.'

'I do. I've tried them on for the girls and they're fab. I'm going to keep them safe until the wedding. I lose earrings all the time. They get caught in my jumpers when I'm taking them off—'

'You're adorable.' She dismissed me with a wave of her hand.

The dismissal was a gift from God, more precious than any rare stone. I can't lie well. I get all loose-lipped and jittery. I could have just said thanks. But instead I had to harp on about the earrings and actually tell fibs. I was 'creating content' because of my inability to say no. I call it 'creating content' because I don't like identifying myself as a liar. But that's what I was.

I had to stop going with the flow, saying yes, being good and nice and palatable just in case I upset someone. Why was it so hard? When would I learn to say, 'No, I don't have holes in my head in which to put these overpriced jewels, but thank you for the gift.'

There was no 'cousin's wedding', or any event that was so important I would get my ears pierced to wear the pearls. I had them done for my communion (yet another 'just because': I had said yes because everyone else was doing it) but I hate earrings so the holes closed up in response to neglect. The girl on the design desk Photoshopped the earrings onto a picture of me she pulled from Facebook and hung it on the wall as a joke. Heather didn't comment but we knew she clocked the earrings. She never asked about them. It would have been beneath her even to remember she'd given them to me.

Christmas rolled around and the earrings gathered dust in my drawer. I was summoned to the office on our final day, after we'd all opened the Kindles we'd been given. Another Brown Thomas bag sat on her desk. She handed it to me with her baby finger. 'A bonus,' she said, without turning fully towards me.

'For what?' I asked, before I remembered she hated to be challenged or questioned.

Instead of answering she extended her arm. I took the bag. 'Thanks so much. I'll open it on Christmas Day, if that's OK. I have a policy of only opening two gifts before Christmas. The Kindle was one.' She smiled and dismissed me. I'd known she'd like me having a 'policy' to restrict the festivities around Christmas.

Back in the kitchen the girls hovered around me. I opened another small velvet pouch. Out rolled two gemstone earrings. Dangly ones this time. 'Oh, my fucking God.'

You get the picture. Every year since then I have received a pair of earrings from that woman because I was too afraid and polite to say no the first time. Now it's *waaaay* too late to let the cat out of the velvet pouch. Gems, gold, silver, fake or possibly real diamonds, all attached to little piercing pins, sit in my drawer as eternal reminders of my weakness and my people-pleasing nature. It was so important for me that this woman approved of me and I stayed in good favour because I refused to show her the truth about me. If I meet her now, I make sure my hair covers my ears. I pretend to have holes in my head rather than make her feel the light discomfort of having made a mistake. I'm the Girl With The Pearl Earring – I haven't read that book but when I googled it it said that the character Griet is hired to be Vermeer's cleaner after he had fired every other cleaner they'd had. She gets the job because she is able to clean his studio without leaving any trace of herself. She leaves everything exactly as it was, making herself, her work and her presence undetectable. She's hired because she can make herself invisible and put Vermeer's need for control ahead of her need to be seen as a real person.

My friends are happy to borrow the earrings for life events. But when I place them back in the drawer I often think that maybe if I'd said no Heather might not have hated or rejected me. She might have given me something I could actually use. Guess I'll never know now. Anyone want to buy some pearl earrings? Like new, never worn. RRP €249.

I sometimes get frustrated when I look back at my early and mid-twenties. I wish I could take myself by the shoulders, shake myself and shout, 'STOP, STEFANIE. JUST STOP. You don't make anyone funnier by being less funny yourself. You don't make anyone greater by making yourself less. Your value is not connected to how agreeable or accommodating you are.' If I had said this to mid-twenties Stefanie in that tone, she would probably have cried. Or, more likely, she would have made some sassy defensive comment, and then, if she made it through the car journey home without breaking down, she would have gone into the shower, turned her face up towards the head and let her tears disappear down the drain with the water.

12

IN MY EARLY TWENTIES, I WAS DANGEROUSLY CLOSE to losing the little voice inside that people call 'your gut' or 'your instinct'. I think of it like this. I would wake up every morning, someone would hand me my 'costume' for the day and I would don it unquestioningly. I had no foresight or concern for the day when I would wake up, naked, and no one would hand me my clothes. What would happen when I walked into a clothes shop for the first time by myself and had to choose? I had no idea of my sense of style, my tastes, my desires, what suited me and what didn't. When the day finally arrived, I floundered around in a metaphorical knitted sweater and clown pants.

In an effort to find out who I was, and what I wanted in life, I had to reassess every aspect of myself to see if it was truly me or something someone had decided for me. From politics to brands of teabag, I had to test the fedora against the beret. I postponed learning about myself until I was too old to be forgiven for 'going through a phase'. I didn't know who I was until I was old enough to know better.

I had started to become trapped inside the story I knew about myself.

I had to start looking at the things I thought were facts about myself to see how many of them held up. Was I 'bubbly'? Did I like roast lamb? Was I the kind of person who prefers to sleep on their side? Was I a true introvert? Or was that just a coping mechanism for all the demands I put on myself to make myself funny and likeable? Was it just a habit from being an only child?

I was exhausted. I believed that my value to the world lay in how accommodating I could be. I gathered platitudes and praise. Once a man asked me what time it was as he passed me on a Dublin street. I looked up at a massive clock on the front of a nearby hotel and told him ten thirty-five. He responded, 'God bless your eyesight,' and walked away. I stood up a little straighter. A man praising my eyesight was enough.

At my lowest point, a generic email offering me 10 per cent off my next purchase in Superdry or Zara made me feel a little more virtuous and worthy. I had a difficult time saying no to things like Black Friday deals, let alone the personal and professional demands being made of me.

During this time I wrapped myself up in the comfort of my best friend Rachel. I kept her abreast of every bloated feeling, every ruined top with my lunch spilled down it. I sent my daily gratitudes to her. I sent her articles 'to be discussed later'. I asked her to watch TV shows so we could dissect them over the phone. As I spread myself thin, like a teaspoon of butter over twenty-eight rice cakes, I constantly returned to Rachel to fill me up again. Reigniting me after I had become quenched by extroversion became Rachel's occupation. There was no room for anything else in her life. And I didn't even notice.

I know a lot of things about my best friend. I know she loves the beach. I know she struggles with the concept of God. I know she burps in public and doesn't feel the need to apologise for it, although she says, 'Excuse me,' when she does it around me. I know she likes to listen to podcasts while she's walking. I know she loves noise-cancelling headphones. I know she doesn't like mixing walking and noise-cancelling headphones because she's afraid of getting hit by traffic. I know she's self-conscious about a little scar above her lip that was the result of a bike crash. I know that no one else can even see the scar but her self-consciousness is adorable.

Every time Rachel's name comes up, I feel the need to give you some more information about her. I love her so much and so ferociously that I'd like to put up huge monuments to our friendship. It feels weird that you don't know everything about her, like I do. Even the way she licks the foil yoghurt top when she opens it is a detail that defines her. She's my best friend, my other half, my soul-mate. Rachel is the person in the world who knows me best and understands me most. We are always in touch with each other. We fill each other in on the details of our lives. If I'm recounting my day to her, it's not a simple case of 'Today I met so-and-so for lunch': she would know that from yesterday. I'm telling her what I ordered from the menu, what I wore, where I sat, whether the hot barista was working . . . I feel as if I live my own life here in Dublin but am simultaneously experiencing Rachel's in New York. If she has an interview or a doctor's appointment, I often have a worry pain, as though I was the one going through it. We're twin-close. We're one-on-the-toilet-one-brushing-teeth kinda close.

I know that Rachel sleeps like the dead, and when she doesn't, she turns into a grumpy toddler you want to hold and rock to sleep. I know she has a curvy spine, which I think is from bending over backwards for people but her physiotherapist disagrees with me. I know she is both ferociously loyal and endlessly forgiving. She is completely committed to the people she loves. I know she is a little bit psychic and has a way of interpreting tarot cards that kind of freaks me out. I know her favourite food is soup and a sandwich, when she's in Ireland. I know that when she's not really listening to me on the phone she'll just repeat the last thing I said in a funny voice. I know she lets me choose the restaurant. I know she doesn't like to have to be the one making decisions. I know she loves crafting and enjoys simpler things than I do. I know that saying no is difficult for her and she wouldn't ever do it lightly. I know that I pushed her too hard for too long and that's why The Conversation had to happen.

'No, Stefanie,' said my best friend Rachel. It came in the form of a sobbing phone call. By the end both of us were crying but at the start it was just Rachel. She was crying because she was afraid. She was scared of my reaction to being told no.

Let me go back a bit.

I'm a nightmare. I am an unmitigated, demanding nightmare. Maybe it's because I'm an only child and I fear being alone. Maybe it's because I'm afraid of being left out, like Blythe. It turned out, in my attempt to keep Rachel close to me, I had ended up like Alison on the beach, or any of the other girls who had a gravitational pull that sucked people into their orbit and kept them there out of force rather than genuine attraction. I might be being too hard on myself here but I feel, out of respect to Rachel's experience, I need to give a cold, hard depiction of just how demanding I'd become.

When Rachel moved to New York I felt like one of my organs had got a Green Card and was moving across the world to get away from me. I took it badly and personally. I didn't want to see her only on holidays when she was trying to fit twelve other people in. I didn't want to have to squeeze four to six months of news into one catch-up hour-long meal in a crowded cheap café in Dublin or New York. I didn't want to feel like I was speed-dating my best friend. I didn't want her to spend weekends getting to know new people. I didn't want to not know what her latest favourite song was, or what new clothing brand she was into, or what ridiculous thing she had seen on her commute to work. I didn't want to have to ask, 'Who's Anna, again?' when she tried to tell me a story about a new colleague. I wanted to know the minutiae of her life, like I did when we lived close together.

Rachel, not wanting me to sever our friendship, amplified her contact with me. We spoke every day, for free, thanks to the internet, and wrote letters. We'd gone on like that for years. Then Rachel met her boyfriend, and when he became her fiancé I started to cling ever closer to her in the fear that I would be demoted as his family and friends became a priority in her life.

I was afraid I would lose her. I had lost my fantasy of what our twenties together would look like. I had already said goodbye to weekend breaks in cheap Ryanair adjacent destinations. I had said farewell to being side by side on sun loungers. I had given up on us living together and going on double dates and having casual lunches that went on for hours. Losing track of time was something I didn't get to do with Rachel now. Assiduously making plans and schedules to maximise our experiences, to make the most memories in the shortest amount of time, became a challenge I felt the need to take on.

Eventually it became too much for her. She rang me that day to tell me, 'No.' It hit me like a metal scooter to the ankle. Perspective disappeared and I was certain I was being abandoned. This is typical Stefanie. I always go to the worst-case scenario. I had started having unfair expectations of Rachel. She has a predilection for people-pleasing like me and had let it go unchecked because she was afraid of losing me too. She was afraid that by saying no to me I would leave. That was the day I learned the lesson. If it had been an episode of *Sabrina*, we would be close to the end of the show when Sabrina has the epiphany and is released from whatever torture she's experiencing because she's finally got the message. I learned that saying no to people won't make them leave you if they want you around. And if they do leave you, they were already looking for a reason to do so.

My recollection of how this went down is a bit blurry. I remember hearing Rachel crying and saying, 'I can't do this any more.' My face got really hot. I could hear my heartbeat in my ears. My stomach felt like I'd eaten sixteen grapefruits and drunk a litre of black coffee. I was raw. Rachel told me she couldn't show up to our friendship like she had been. She was meeting my expectations, and whether or not they were too high was beside the point: she just couldn't do it. Tactful as she always is, she made a huge effort not to assign blame to either of us. She didn't say, 'You are too demanding.' She was careful to take the responsibility as hers and say, 'I can't do what you're asking me to do.' I'd been asking her to commit to voice-messaging me every morning. She had been doing it for a few months but she explained she would wake up anxious about forgetting to send it to me immediately and what would happen if she missed a day. She told me she felt like she was choking. I was the first thing she thought of every morning but not in a good way. She was making me happy before she had even boiled the kettle for herself.

I fought my instincts to get defensive. It was easy because she wasn't attacking me. I listened. I cried. And eventually I spoke. 'Do you not want to be friends any more?'

She cried even more. 'No, I do, but you probably don't want to be friends with me now.'

'Of course I do. We just have to find another way.'

I sobbed and told her my silliest, most outrageous fears. I can't remember the ones I actually mentioned, but the ones I felt so intensely have left their mark. I was afraid she was trying to get rid of me to make more space for her fiancé. I was afraid our lives were so different and distant that soon we would be past each other's horizons and invisible to each other. I was afraid we'd never sleep in the same bed again and fall asleep scratching each other's forearms. I was afraid Nana would die and Rachel wouldn't be there to hold me together. I was afraid that the person I thought loved me most was about to abandon me and prove my greatest fear: that I was not enough to keep anyone in my life. I was afraid she would highlight the fact that I was unlovable. I spoke some of these words to Rachel. Some she will read for the first time in this book.

Instead of flying off the handle and letting my anxiety manifest as anger, I let myself be vulnerable and afraid. I let myself be Little Stef. I let Little Stef voice her worries to her best friend, and we were able to listen and hear each other. Rachel was crying because she was afraid. We were the same. She was afraid her 'No' would make me leave her and I was afraid her 'No' meant she was leaving me. Neither was true.

By the end of the call – the phone showed 02:14:06 when we eventually hung up – I sensed that Rachel would never leave me. We had pushed past some sort of threshold. We were like two children flashing their naked bodies at each other just to prove they both had the same parts. Rachel was the braver of us because she went first. Her courage saved our friendship. And my life. That was when I realised I had to start saying no to people. I couldn't keep saying yes to things I didn't want to do or simply couldn't do. I had to change how I related to the world because choking myself to death at the hands of other people was not an option. If Rachel was brave enough to tell her best friend no, then I was brave enough to tell Helen in the accounts department that it wasn't OK for her to fuck up my invoice for the fourth month running.

This was a new me. It was a new Stefanie: she had the solid comfort of having a best friend who would be there for her at every step of the way. Having someone to call you out when you're being shitty or demanding or demeaning or unreasonable means you can go about your life knowing you'll never be too far off course. It's the difference between having only a start and finish line while orienteering or having way-stations every few miles so you never get lost.

Having Rachel as my personal cheerleader and being one for her is the greatest reinforcement in my life. She is part of my identity. She and I are an 'us'. It feels delicious when I hear her saying to people, '*We* haven't seen the final series of *Girls.*' When she calls us a 'we' it's the feeling of belonging that comes with that word that I never want to lose. I love the conspiratorial joy that comes from staring at each other in a group when someone says something ridiculous, and knowing we have both clocked and pocketed it 'to be discussed later'. Weathering that 'No' with Rachel and turning it into a shared mythology in which we embellish it and laugh about it, is part of the DNA of our friendship. There is a pre- and post-no phase of our lifespan together. The post-no is endlessly joyous.

We use that conversation as our litmus test, yardstick and training ground. When we have to say 'No' now, we go back to that one and dissect it from a different angle. 'OK, so this time you're me and your boss is you.' Rachel will coach me through it again and again.

Rachel and I had reached a crisis point. For her, we had either to confront it and try to fix it or leave each other. By working through it we were released into the world knowing that no 'No' would break us up because that one hadn't. I was ready to start giving no a go.

The ReNOssance

13

WHEN PEOPLE APOLOGISE BUT DON'T KNOW WHAT they're saying sorry for, it's offensive, meaningless and irritating. It would take me a while to realise this applied to saying no. I knew that I needed to start doing so. But that's pretty useless information unless you know how to put it into practice, or why you're saying no. I started putting this puzzle together in my early twenties. Learning I needed to say no was one thing. Learning *how* was another.

After I graduated from drama school in 2010, no one was casting me, no one was saying yes to me. I couldn't progress without other people's permission and no one seemed willing to give it. I started to write plays for myself to perform in, not least because I seemed to be the only person willing to put myself on stage. I dug into the well of my past experiences and used what I found to lift me out of the funk I was in.

I was full of doubt and fear and felt like I was breaking all sorts of rules. Little Stef, the still small voice inside me, told me it was OK to do it. She said it didn't matter if I failed because no one had asked me to write something in the first place so nobody was expecting anything from me. I wrote in secret. I worried constantly that I was being self-indulgent, narcissistic and arrogant by writing about my life. I wrote a lot in rhyme because I felt if I crafted my thoughts in verse it would be harder to criticise me for being self-obsessed. I fictionalised parts to try to prevent people accusing me of thinking I was more interesting than I actually was. I didn't think I was particularly interesting but I did think I was chronically unique: I had been struck down with the incurable illness of originality, which meant no one could or would ever understand me. I wrote to try to make sense of my world. (It's still why I write but I learned very quickly that I am the opposite of unique and that, actually, my experiences are almost identical to those of most Irish women my age.)

During the writing process – before I even knew I was in a process – I would go to the back of a café in Temple Bar. It had a janky little smoking area with two seats where nobody ever went. That little corner of Dublin was a Petri dish. In its damp, hot atmosphere, ideas had time to incubate without the fear of criticism the outside world threatened. I showed up every day, took my seat in the garden area with my coffee, lit my cigarette and purged my life into my laptop. It was a small but radical act of defiance. I was saying no. No to the tradition of calling myself a writer only after I'd been published. No to feeling like a failed actor because I had changed lanes. No to the pressure to buy more than one coffee because I was afraid of taking up space. No to the big voice inside me that screamed, 'YOU ARE RIDICULOUS AND THIS IS GOING TO FAIL.' No to imposter syndrome. No to the culture of 'not enough'. No to fucking all of it.

I texted Rachel – I'm doing it, pal! She cheered me on from across the Atlantic. I wished every day that she could be beside me as I typed. Every syllable that came out of me screamed to run past her for approval. I controlled my urge to be resentful that she wasn't attached to my hip. The irony is that if she had been there I would never have written. Rachel and I are highly skilled in the arts of dual procrastination and distraction. Her absence was one of the strongest supports she could have given me. She cheered me on via text and email.

I was a writer. I had something to write. I gave myself deadlines. At a certain point I knew I needed the sensible, non-distracting presence of someone I could trust to be an audience for the play before it had a real audience. I had a gorgeous, generous, genius friend named Jack, the only person I trusted with the delicate fragments of my life I was piecing together. I would travel out to his folks' house in Ranelagh and read my play with him, to him, for him. I trusted and valued his opinion. I knew he wouldn't placate me but, more importantly, Jack is not someone who sees other people's success as a challenge to his own. He doesn't elevate himself by criticising others. He is a gentleman, a well-read, observant, articulate gem.

I travelled weekly to lay my brittle creation at his feet. He handled it with the same care I did. He knew how precious, half-formed things can easily be talked out of existence. We were like parents handing a premature baby. Gentle and amazed and scared.

I was a writer. I had a play to write. I had a purpose. With this purpose came the responsibility of executing it. I had no boss: I was the only one who cared if the thing ever got written. Well, me and Jack. This self-driven aspect of the project was how I learned to say no again. If I hadn't started to say no to many of the things that summer offered me, I would never have finished the play. I had no time for small-talk, lunches or birthday drinks that turned into birthday weekends and expanded into birthday weeks.

By the end of the summer I had a play. It was the opportunity cost of everything I had missed that summer. Each monologue had a correlating concert, birthday, comedy gig, opening night, closing night, weekend staycation that I had forgone. I am sure it would probably have been completed even if I'd gone to some of the events in 2011. Maybe it wouldn't, though. I was totally uncompromising in my ambition to get that play finished. I held on to it like a lifeline. In a way, it *was* a lifeline. I was carving a career path that summer. I knew I wasn't going to sustain a full-time career as an actor so I had to find a new way of living. I wrote for Jack. My inner circle closed around me, like a swimming ring. It was keeping me afloat as I drifted on the choppy waters of a potential identity crisis. Waves of fear, waves of irrelevance, waves of being dismissed and overlooked and unheard crashed around me, but I stayed typing in my swimming ring. And at the end I floated onto the shore with a play that I now needed someone to say yes to programming at their venue or festival.

People are impressed by self-starters. If you can show you're willing to make stuff happen, they see investment in you as a risk worth taking. Roise Goan at the Dublin Fringe Festival and Tom Creed of the Cork Midsummer Festival gave me my first yes, which has made every other yes more possible. At the 2012 Dublin Fringe Festival I produced and staged my first play. It was called *Our Father*, funded by myself and my friends, who GoFunded Me.

The play had a cast of four. A new director and three actors I had never worked with before became four friends, who replaced some who had dropped away when I turned down multiple offers to activities I didn't have time for. Someone should do a PhD on friendship thresholds. I want to know where the point of no return is. Because there is one. There are only so many noes that a friendship can sustain.

When I was saying yes to things I didn't I want, I was building a low-level resentment towards people and myself. Once I started writing, I had a new priority, and by focusing on it, I could say no to anything that would distract me. Having a purpose absolved me of the guilt I would usually feel and gave me an excuse that was difficult to poke holes in.

It's easy to say no when you haven't time to do what's being asked. It doesn't cause others too much hardship to say no to a Wednesday beach trip when they should be at work. During the rehearsal period and performance run at the theatre festival, saying no wasn't hard because I couldn't possibly have said yes. It was the noes while I was writing and after the festival that were really difficult.

There's nothing worse than the anti-climax on the Monday after your show ends. You go from being in an hour-to-hour routine with the same people every day to nothing. During the run, your food schedule, clothing, TV viewing and phone use are dictated by the show. You see the same people in the same dressing room every day. You wear the same thing and say the same lines every day. A routine of post-show wind-down or blow-out develops. Then it's over and it's as if the stage manager hands you back all of those hours to fill again. You forget what life was like before the show.

I had said no to so many people for so long that, on the Monday morning after *Our Father*, I had no one to hang out with. I had loads of time.

I went concave from fear and loneliness. I had some funding applications to do, a national tour of the show to piece together, but the FOMO was overwhelming. People all over Facebook were hanging out without me and I was ringing theatres in rural Ireland trying to get them to say yes to me. It took all of my strength to stick to my guns and stay in my no.

Saying yes to invites was the easy option. It would have soothed me to spend time with people who wanted to be in my company rather than continuously running on the hamster wheel of rejection, trying to put the tour together. But I did it.

I kept saying no to invites, leaving space in my life for those I wanted to say yes to me: the programme managers of the venues I was calling. Each no left space for someone else's yes.

Each no was to a different offer but I was invariably saying the same thing.

No, that's not a priority for me.

No, I'm not able to do that.

No is a complete sentence.

I got my first yes on a Tuesday. I jumped up and down in my living room. I had no one to celebrate the victory with but that didn't matter. I had so much energy – that was one thing to strike me when I started saying no. I also realised I'm painfully shy. The characters I create are not shy. And sometimes I felt like I was playing a character. Saying yes to everything was an energy, personality and charisma drain. But on that Tuesday I was making things happen for myself. I had objectives, goals and values, and finally my life was lining up with what I wanted. I had felt like I was stuck, like my life was totally out of my control. I played games like The Sims and thought, If only I could control my life like I'm controlling this little avatar's. And then I realised I *can*. I'd heard people saying things like 'You do you' or 'Be true to yourself' but I always felt those were profound answers to profound problems. In fact, they were just more eloquent versions of 'Say no.'

Someone smarter than I am once told me that people come into your life for a reason, a season or a lifetime. When I heard that I railed against it because I have a natural fear of being abandoned and like to think that everyone I care about will be in my life for ever. The further I went along my new path of saying no, the more I realised that having certain people in your life fleetingly can be a blessing.

One friend was in my life for exactly a season: summer 2013. Some people argue that summer is June, July and August. When I was in school we learned that summer was May, June and July, while August was the start of autumn. I still remember the teacher drawing a line from the 'Au' in August to the 'Au' in autumn to drill it into our heads. Either way, it was mostly sunny for the three months I knew Maria. I met her during an international arts conference in Dublin. We became very close very quickly. Intense, immediate closeness had become part of my MO at college and drama school. I think I felt that, if I shared all my past, my fears, my jokes and my Diet Cokes with someone, I could fake the genuine connection I had with Rachel. With Rachel the connection is a rope made of fibres that have grown, twisted and wrapped around each other over years of shared experience, long conversations on night-time drives and endless debates about whether caffeine affects your sleep if it's all you ever drink.

I know now that you can't fake a shared history. It's like trying to grow a sister or even a twin. You can make it look genuine from the outside but you both know it's an act. Maria wanted us to do everything together, which was great in May and June because I was at a loose end. Once mid-July came around I had rehearsals. *Solpadeine Is My Boyfriend* was premiering at the Dublin Fringe Festival. It was my second play, and a one-woman show. It needed every ounce of attention my millennial brain could muster.

I'd told Maria I wouldn't be around as much as I had been but I'd happily meet her for dinner after rehearsals. Initially she agreed and didn't protest at all. Then it was as if she was stricken with memory loss. Every day she would text me a new offer: *Hey, want to get out to the RSA exhibit today?*

The first few times I found different ways of reminding her that I was rehearsing. *We're working on the opening scenes today so I can't, sorry* or *The lighting designer is coming in today – soz.* Those messages might have led her to believe that if I hadn't planned a specific engagement I would have been available to her. Eight days into rehearsals, after eight invites I couldn't attend, I got a bit clearer.

Fancy checking out the Leprechaun Museum and getting Mexican food?

Maria, I am in rehearsals all day, every day from now until the show opens in three weeks. I told you this.

Sent. I could see she had read it. No response. My stomach lurched. Had I been too harsh? I sent another text: *I'm sorry if I didn't make that clear. I'd love to do stuff with you but I'm chained to the rehearsal room.* No response. I checked my phone every hour. I might as well have gone with Maria to the Leprechaun Museum because my mind was with her for the rest of the day. And the following day. That was at least five years ago now and I still haven't heard back. Evidently, eight is the number of noes that a friendship can sustain.

I swung wildly on the pendulum from being the world's greatest yes-woman to saying no indiscriminately. For the first time, I was getting a handle on it. Having a goal, a primary purpose and my own priorities was my compass. I now had a test to decide what was worth saying yes to: did it take me away from my goal? If so, no.

When the play finished, I tried to make myself a list of criteria for saying no. I wanted a kind of policy document, a set of guidelines, so I could feel removed from the emotion of it. I took my cue from a Dublin City Council parking-enforcement guy. My parking ran out and I came back to my car just as he was putting the clamp on my front wheel. I begged him to remove it. I offered him friendship, a great TripAdvisor review, a dinner invitation to Nando's. I think I even offered him my kidney. He was having none of it. He told me he had a set of guidelines he had to follow. It wasn't his decision: he had no power or control. I know he probably *could* have used his discretion if he'd really wanted to but, for whatever reason, he didn't need a new friend or a free chicken-wing meal, so he stuck to his schtick of being powerless to operate outside the protocols in place. It was very difficult to argue with him. So, I followed his example and set out my own policy.

Now I can see my rules are too black and white, but at the time I needed something simple and clear.

1. Work comes first. If I get invited to something, or asked to do something that takes me away from my work, it's a non-negotiable no.

2. Nothing after 6 p.m.

3. Nothing outside Dublin that isn't work-related.

4. Nothing in a bar/club/pub.

5 Nothing that takes me away from Nana or Mam.

6. Nothing hosted in a venue with a capacity over twenty.

7. Nothing that keeps me awake at night or is the first thing my mind worries about in the morning.

When I had something to write it was easy to say no, but keeping the rules without the reason behind them was bizarre and isolating.

For a few years of my life I lived by these rules. I called them policies to make them seem more official and less petty. When I started saying no and got a taste for the freedom it could bring, I over-corrected my yes-woman behaviour and said no to *everything*. For a few years I existed in an ever-shrinking social circle. I was like airport security during a period of high threat. I saw every invitation, request and offer as a potential explosive. 'Do you want to meet for coffee?' was a vessel of liquid or an aerosol over 100ml. 'Will you do me a favour?' was a sharp object. 'What're you up to this weekend?' was a bag I hadn't packed myself. 'Can you drop me to town on your way?' was a Samsung Galaxy S7, likely to combust at any moment. My rules became too restrictive and uncompromising. But at the start, when I wanted to write my plays and be productive, I needed to be that way. The period of over-correcting showed me I had to find a balance.

It was a massive shift from the girl who measured her

worth in how accommodating she could be. I confused many people during the time I spent 'finding myself'. There was nothing 'typical' about me any more. Everything that had defined me was up for debate. Even close friends mistook my introversion for me being unfriendly. I had done such a good job of always showing up with a smile and being entertaining that people thought that was who I was, as though being 'great craic' and 'the entertainment' were extra chromosomes woven into my DNA. Once I didn't have it in me to pretend any more, some people dropped me. I don't blame them. It's the relationship equivalent of buying a television only to bring it home and find it's a radio. You have a right to return something if it's not what you signed up for. I let them go to find the technicolour entertainment they wanted.

Others were content with the picture-but-no-sound me. Maybe they knew that in certain environments they'd get a glimpse of colourful Stefanie. Maybe they were self-assured enough to know that it was not their failing if I showed up in quiet mode. Maybe they preferred me that way.

14

WHEN YOU START SAYING NO, IT HELPS TO KNOW WHO you are, your personality type, and the kinds of things you enjoy so that when offers come in you can categorise them quickly.

When I started saying no, I didn't know what I actually enjoyed and what I would prefer to avoid, and because I didn't know, I had no way of differentiating enjoyable from exhausting activities. This led me to the blanket no policy, which didn't serve me.

Now I ask myself, 'Would I absolutely hate this because of

who I am as a person?' That necessitates knowing who I am, a whole other matrix of complexity, because I'm changing all the time. I make a definitive statement, like 'I don't eat dairy',* then two days later I'm elbow deep in Skyr yoghurt and having an identity crisis. Being definitive about anything is a bit restrictive but there are some things I know and from that I can make a list of things which are part of who I am.

1. I can't do small-talk.

2. I'm terribly sarcastic.

3. I can't 'wonder' about something without finding the answer.

4. I'm intensely focused on my goals.

5. In communication I am direct.

6. I expend large amounts of energy trying to fit in.

7. I am happy in my own company.

8. I like meeting people but they drain me after a short time.

9. I would rather have no Wi-Fi than ask for the password.

10. I would rather hold it than ask where the bathroom is.

---

* because of my asthma – but who can resist froyo.

11. I smile and nod in understanding when I hear people talk about being introverts.

12. I don't know how to respond to 'How are you?' when it's used as a greeting.

13. I'm bored and anxious in crowds.

14. I'm a cynical idealist.

15. I'm ferociously loyal.

16. I do not love easily but when I do it is specific and deep.

These are not all traits I would choose if I got to create myself, like at those Build-A-Bear Workshops. I'd like to swap some of my hatred of crowds for a thirst for adventure. But that's not how life works and Build-A-Bear is a problematic model on which to base human evolution. I am who I am, and as long as I know it, I can try to honour it and make my life as happy, joyous and drama-free as possible. What are your Build-A-Bear traits?

15

ONCE I STARTED TO REALISE WHO I WAS, I WAS ABLE to put time and consideration into what I would say no to. Scrutinising every option seemed overwhelming. The only way to eat an elephant is one bite at a time, or so they say, but I felt as if I was being asked to eat a whole herd. If I was asked to go to the cinema, I faced a game-show level of questioning. I felt like I was taking deep breaths in cold weather. It stung and made me lightheaded. The questions rushed in.

Do I want to go? Too big a question to ask: there were too many variables.

Do I really like the person inviting me, or am I just friends with them because I've always been friends with them? If I met this person for the first time today would we have anything in common on which to build a friendship?

Will I like the movie I'm being invited to? Will I really like it, or do I just think I enjoy chick flicks because I've been targeted due to my age and gender and have developed a taste for them based purely on exposure? Will there be popcorn? Can I eat the popcorn? AM I SAYING YES TO THE CINEMA ONLY FOR THE POPCORN?

By the time I'd come to a conclusion, I'd be sweating, shaking and exhausted because of the sheer effort of making a decision and the film would likely be long over – maybe not even showing in cinemas any more. I had to pare it *waaaay* back and keep it simple.

My first 'considered' noes were very small things.

No, I won't answer that call right now. I'll keep writing instead.

No, I won't have this argument again. I'll just walk away.

No, I won't eat that thing now. I'll enjoy my dinner more if I don't.

No, I won't put off calling Mam. She'll be dead one day.

16

PEOPLE SAY THAT MAKING A DECISION TO CHANGE IS the hardest and biggest part of the change. That is so not true when it comes to saying no. I had decided to start taking back some control of my life, how I spent my time, who I spent it with and where, but that was simple compared to saying the word directly to someone's face or even to their phone.

Early in this new phase of my life, as though the universe wanted to test me, a series of invitations came along at the same time. I'd gone off into the big bad world with my criteria and in came five requests: a wedding, a work gig at a music festival, two social nights out and a date.

Because of *course* the universe couldn't have eased me into it. Oh, no.

This wedding wasn't as difficult to say no to as many have been. I was invited as a plus one to the wedding of two people I barely knew. In any other circumstances, I wouldn't have had to think twice. The issue was that I was being invited as a last-minute stand-in for a boyfriend.

My friend Debbie and her other half had been planning to go together but had since broken up. Debbie was too afraid to tell the bride that she wasn't feeling up it, and she sort of believed she could find another boyfriend in the few weeks between the break-up and the wedding. When Mr Right didn't pop up in a tuxedo ready to accompany her, I was called in as the 'old reliable'. I felt so bad at the idea of saying no. I knew she'd been banking on me saying yes. How was she to know I'd been changing policy documents in secret in the weeks she was on the prowl for a date? I felt I should have told her sooner that I was changing as a person and I wasn't going to be ICE friend any more. I was lots of people's ICE friend – In Case of Emergency.

I said no to the wedding. I fully believed I was saying no to being able to call Debbie a friend any more. I thought she would hate me. But I explained my new policy – in the least crazy way possible – and she got it. Instead of being angry and shouting at me, she became soft and vulnerable, and asked me to help her say no to attending the wedding. In 2.5 seconds I had not only become someone who could say no, but *someone people were asking to help them learn to say no*. It was bizarre. But we did it. And the world didn't fall apart. The wedding went ahead, no one missed Debbie on the day, and everyone lived happily ever after. It turns out that real friends don't want to force you into something you don't want to do! Who knew?

The second offer was harder to say no to because it didn't fit neatly into any of my criteria. A music festival would have been a very simple and clear no. With a capacity of upwards of ten thousand people, and its location outside Dublin, it was a no-brainer. That was before you even looked at the 6 p.m. and pub/club criteria. The issue was that this was a work offer. It was money. It was an offer from a person I enjoy working with and it had come in through my publicist, all things that triggered the yes-woman in me. These were people I wanted to be helpful and easy-going with. I took time to think about it. Buying time became one of the most useful tools when saying no. It was a new skill I had to develop. If I knew I wanted to say no, but needed to pluck up the courage, the gall or the tact, I had learned that asking for a little time to think really helped. A simple 'Can I come back to you on that?' gave me a non-specific amount of time to make up my mind.

If someone comes back and says they need an answer *right away* it's very easy to say no – you're clearly being put under pressure. So, if they won't let you come back to them, it's an immediate no – and they won't be surprised.

Having bought myself more time, the following days were a hazy stream of anxious morning thoughts and sleepless night-time fears about what would happen at the festival. I came back to my list. The anxiety tipped the scale for me. It felt wrong. I sat at my laptop and wrote a ridiculously long email to my publicist, Aileen. I almost used graphs to explain to her why I had to say no, how sorry I was and begged her to pass on my apologies. I asked her if she thought I would ever work again or if this made me a bad person. I finished the email with another apology and a sad-face emoji. I read the email fifteen times and pressed send. Immediately, I got a response: *Cool. I'll go back to them with that. Have a great day.*

I couldn't believe that was it. That was it? No disaster? No accusations of being difficult to work with? It was a while before I allowed my suspicion to turn into relief. I was in suspense, wondering when my boundaries were going to blow up in my face.

Saying no to the social events wasn't a big deal. Once I'd said no, my friends laughed and said they were glad I was finally putting an end to the torture for myself. They said I looked so uncomfortable sometimes when we were out, but they always invited me because they didn't want me to feel left out. I told them that their invites had felt like a summons. We all laughed and agreed that they wouldn't ask me any more and I wouldn't feel left out. Now I meet them for brunch or coffee – usually one at a time.

Saying no to the date was trickier because I felt the same guilt I had with Debbie. I realised too late into the coffee meeting that it was a date. I had been texting this guy and thought he was funny and smart. I'm terrible at reading people so I didn't pick up on the flirting or that the offer of 'grabbing a coffee' was not as casual and haphazard as he had made it sound. As he asked the waitress for his third top-up I realised I was in deep. I didn't know how to get out of the situation.

I couldn't say no because there was nothing concrete to say no to, yet the longer it went on the deeper into discomfort I sank. So, I turned casual. I started calling him 'buddy' and 'mate'. Anyone observing from outside would have thought I was having some kind of stroke because my behaviour changed so dramatically and so quickly.

He got confused. Fair enough. In response, he asked if he could take me to dinner the following night. He was making a very clear offer of a date because he was confused by my bizarre behaviour. This was my chance to say no. I clammed up. The heat spread up my neck, along the sides of my face and into my hair. The guilt and fear were like a rash. I was certain that if I bruised his ego by saying no now, he would accuse me of leading him on, of teasing him and being some kind of Medusa. I didn't have to say no. He knew from my behaviour. He was definitely annoyed – he left without paying for the coffees. I picked up the bill and took it as my penalty: a fine for being misleading. Now I see it as a small price to pay for sparing myself an evening on a date I didn't want to be on.

17

HANGING OUT WITH OLD PEOPLE IS A GREAT WAY TO SEE 'saying no' in action. My nana doesn't do anything she doesn't want to do. And, because she's ninety-one, no one makes her. She suits herself. She asks for what she wants, pushes back on what she doesn't and isn't afraid of seeming 'difficult'. She will ask for a seat in the middle of a grocery store queue. She will ask someone to turn down the volume if it's uncomfortably loud in a restaurant. In the same restaurant she will send back her meal if it's not to her taste. She doesn't know how many goddamn meals she has left – her life is literally too short to eat a bad steak. She got a hospital appointment which was scheduled for her ninetieth birthday. She'd been waiting for it for months but she just picked up the phone and made them reschedule.

One afternoon, I called into the house and asked, 'Nana, I'm writing my book and I'm wondering is there anything you do out of obligation that you'd rather say no to?'

She thought about it – or, at least, she went silent for a time as she served herself her salmon darne with baby potatoes.

Her list of priorities in that moment looked like:

1. Eat dinner.

2. Watch favourite daytime chat-show.

3.   Don't be harassed by your grandchild looking to cannibalise your life for her latest book.

'I don't have time to think about that now, Stefanie. I want to eat my dinner and relax in peace with Maura and Daithí.'

See? Zero fucks given.

18

MY PAL DEE HAD A BIRTHDAY WHILE I WAS WRITING this book. I went to several shops looking for a card for her and noticed a pattern I wanted vehemently to say no to: forced or feigned sentimentality.

I haven't been to card shops in years because I fundamentally disagree with pre-made cards. My mother owned a stationery shop when I was growing up and she knew all the codes on the back of cards – the ones that relate to price. If we went to visit people in hospital or in their homes and they had cards out on display, I'd notice her doing a sub-perceptible glance at the backs to see the codes. I don't know if it was an occupational curiosity or a way to judge how much people cared that Mary got well soon, but I found it unsettling. I also think that, for the biggest events of your life, cards shouldn't be generic, with a message a copy-writer wrote years ago to be bland and multi-purpose. As I wandered through the shopping centre, I wondered whether card shops had changed while I wasn't looking. I know there are online sites where you can design your own but I didn't have time for one of those because Dee's birthday was on Thursday and this was Monday evening.

First, there's no clearer gender divide than in card shops. Half the shop was pink and lavender and half was blue and orangey. The shiny, glittery, embossed 'DAD', 'MAM', 'MUM', 'SISTER', '50', '60', '90' screamed at me from the entrance. I passed the key-rings and mugs, which had all been baptised with Christian names. I don't even bother looking any more because I know from experience they NEVER have ones that say 'Stefanie'. Goddamn *ph* monopoly!

I have boycotted Mothers' Day since my mother turned over a card I had bought so she could see the price code on the back. I was annoyed that the company had a code that seemed to put a price on my annual appreciation of my mother. Now I get her a present and write the note on the wrapping paper. I see it as saving the planet. But I know she loves cards because she goes out of her way to get one for Nana that says 'Mam' and not 'Mum'. I don't know if my mother is aware that Nana couldn't give a hoot if the card called her 'Genetic Incubator': she appreciates the effort. I go to the 'mother' section to see if I can find one without a code, or perhaps the codes have changed now Mam's been out of the stationery game so long. I get to the pink-hued section of cards and stand before them. I couldn't in good conscience buy one for my mother. The greetings were all based on and propagating the same underlying assumption. *You are a better mother if you sacrifice yourself, put other people's needs before yours, and never say no.*

I had to take a second. I leaned on a display of fridge magnets, which glamorised alcoholism. 'It's wine o'clock.' And 'Keep Calm and Drink Wine'. 'Zero to Naked in 1.5 bottles', 'The Key to My Heart' (with a picture of a bottle-opener), 'You had me at Merlot' and the Christmas-themed 'Prosec-ho-ho-ho'.

I stared at the cards. The sweet, floral, italic messages on some said:

You gave up so much for us.

You sacrificed yourself.

You went without so we wouldn't have to.

You were the kindest, most generous role-model.

One incredibly virtuous one looked more like a mass card and included a quote: 'A mother is a person who, seeing there are only four pieces of the pie for five people, promptly announces she never did care for pie.' Tenneva Jordan.

Where are the cards that thank mothers for giving their kids healthy boundaries, for teaching that you can be loved without being a martyr?

It's not that my mam was never a self-sacrificing people-pleaser. Of course she went without so that I could have Sylvanian Families and endless Super Nintendo games, but is that really the thing I want to thank her for? No.

I need a card for my mam that says:

Thanks for teaching me to be strong.

Thank you for showing me that I have to get up early and go to work.

Thank you for showing me how to be an entrepreneur.

Thank you for showing me that failure won't kill me.

Thank you for teaching me how to stand my ground.

Thank you for letting me see that being single is not a character defect or a flaw.

Thank you for showing me that I am all I need.

Thank you for speaking up, and teaching me the benefits of being uncompromising.

Thank you for taking all those lie-ins so I don't feel bad when I do it now.

Where are *those* cards? Selflessness and martyrdom are not aspirational traits. People-pleasing is not admirable. Can we do something to change this?

The dad cards were different. They thanked fathers for 'the genes and the good looks', 'for teaching me to play football', 'for showing me how to be strong'. They had bold, sharp fonts to tell the dad 'You are my motivation for every step I take.'

It seems it's deviating from a social norm to be a strong and assertive woman but it's commended for men. This is apparently set out as an expectation for us long before our X chromosomes double. Women who know what they want and set out to get it are perceived as threatening. If you want to be liked and want something else as well, like a career, it's a tricky little spot.

If you were the type of woman greetings cards describe, you'd be 'so nice' or 'infinitely kind'. You'd be described by sentences like:

She'd do anything for you.

She's always there for me.

She's the softest shoulder to cry on.

I'd trust her with my life.

I'd turn to her in a crisis.

So basically all you get for your life is other people's bullshit, tears and life crises.

Is that the life you want? Is that the life anyone wants? The woman that these cards describe is condemned to a life that looks like a Greek mythological punishment. The Hallmark Woman – I can see her now. She is always in the process of following her dreams – let's say she wants to be a writer. She is cursed to be finishing the last chapter of her novel when some friend calls her with a need that she must meet. Other people's wants and needs come before hers for eternity. But the good news is that at the end of her life everyone can choose from the greatest selection of cards applicable to her.

I now have an app on my phone where I can put a greeting on one of my photos, type in the address and someone gets it as a postcard in two to three days. It's brilliant. I'm going to make one for Mam for next Mothers' Day.

Dear Mam,
Thank you for asking for directions in front of me so
I know that even grown-ups get lost sometimes
This card cost €5.99 including postage.
I love you €5.99's worth.
Stef xx

I picked up a card for Dee that said 'To my ex-husband on your wedding day' because I reckoned that card would sit on the shelf for years without ever being bought and I felt bad for it. I also knew Dee would find it hilarious. I wrote the card, put it in the envelope, then remembered she'd moved house and I didn't have her new address. I thought texting her to get the address would spoil the surprise of getting a birthday card. And with an expectation of getting something in the post, a cheap blank card with a little note from me in it would be disappointing so I didn't send it. But it's the thought that counts, right? Happy birthday, Dee. X

19

BEFORE I STARTED, I FELT SAYING NO WOULD THREATEN my relationships. I was often afraid it would be met with fury or resentment, which would lead to some awful consequence for me.

I'm a big proponent of tradition and ritual. I find comfort and a sense of belonging in the continuous repetition of a task, event or habit. I have lots of traditions, and my close friends are always aware that if we do the same thing more than three times they may be inadvertently roping themselves into a new one. Here are some of my favourites.

Rachel lives in New York, so she and I tend to spend time together in short, intense bursts. When we're in New York we have a tradition of wearing matching clothing and going shopping together. We watch nostalgic movies and become temporary chiropractors, cracking each other's backs and taking turns to massage each other. Twice now we've cleared out Rachel's wardrobe and donated a bunch of stuff to Goodwill so I'm really hoping this can become a thing.

Mam and I have a tradition of going to the same coffee place when she comes to Dublin every other weekend. It's totally out of our way but we love the coffee and it's a thing now so we're sticking to it. We also have a tradition of spending the June bank-holiday weekend together somewhere warm.

Nana and I have the long-standing tradition of doing the *Sunday Business Post* cryptic crossword together. She waits for me to help her finish it, and if she happens to have 'a good run' and gets through it without me, I'm a little peeved. It doesn't happen very often – our two brains are better than one. We're a team.

I have a tradition with another friend of going to Nando's for our respective birthdays. We used to go once a month but as we get older it's harder to make the monthly slot so we have committed to never letting the birthday arrangement slip. If we can grab chicken wings any other time, we'll take it as a bonus.

I have a tradition of texting my monthly horoscope to a fellow Taurean so we can dissect it together.

I once texted the Boy Housemate in September and asked him if I could book him in to watch *The X Factor* with me.

He knows me better than I know myself so he said no, aware that it would mean committing to spending every weekend in Dublin, with me, for the next four months until the final.

A grown-up in my life has adopted the tradition of emailing me the *New York Times* crossword puzzle each day. I don't always have time to solve it but there's a closeness and a belonging that goes hand in hand with the sound of the email pinging in my phone.

At Christmas I have billions of traditions with different people. The Boy Housemate and I have a tradition of decorating the house together while watching *Home Alone*. We set aside a whole day for it. Nana and I have the tradition of watching *The Snowman*. Our family has a tradition of visiting Nana's neighbours on Christmas Eve and Christmas Day to play gin rummy and eat what they call 'nibbles'. I have my own tradition of getting up early on St Stephen's Day, going for a walk around Castleknock when everyone is still asleep, then going to check out the sales, by myself with my headphones on. Rachel did the shopping part of this once but hated it so much that she vowed never to do it again, lest I rope her into a tradition. Christmas just wouldn't be Christmas without these tiny familiar punctuations.

Except it would.

Because things change.

Christmas, or life, just goes on regardless.

I have had to release my grip on some traditions and although it felt awful at first – like trying to write with your non-dominant hand – you get used to it.

Mam and I used to take her friend's kids to a Christmas fair in Cork City every year. We had a highly structured tradition of going for dinner, then to the toy shop, then queuing for an abhorrent length of time to ride the Big Wheel, which terrified the kids but never enough to break the tradition. This tradition fizzled out in a flurry of missed calls and rain checks. The kids got older and it wasn't so cool to go on a Big Wheel. Mam and their mother drifted apart until one year we realised it wasn't going to happen and that was it. We couldn't make it work and one missed tradition is enough to break the cycle and destroy the ritual. I still feel the absence of that little night when Christmas comes around, and whenever I see the decorations go up on Cork's Grand Parade, I smile. I'm remembering the excited puffs of air escaping from the six-year-old: he was holding his breath in fear and anticipation as our cage on the Big Wheel rose higher and he thought he might glimpse Santa doing a recce of the Cork sky.

Some traditions don't just fade out. When you start saying no to things, or people, the traditions you held with them can break and be scattered across your life, like reflective glass on a black road after a car crash.

I had a friend once, let's call him Derick. We had been friends for years. We had so many shared habits and traditions they were hard to identify because they had become part of us. We started our tradition of jumping at the word 'jump' every time it came on the Girls Aloud track, but eventually I found myself doing it when I was by myself. I still do. Other little things – sayings, phrases, sharing a Double Decker bar (I liked the top half, he liked the crunchy part) – became so ingrained in us that they were almost personality traits rather than the quirks of a friendship. I had never said no to Derick – I had never had any reason to. But in 2015, when I took up a new no, to drinking and eating sugar, my friendship with Derick took a massive hit. Derick took my no to sugar as a no to him. Our friendship didn't have a sugar-free option. For the first few weeks, every time we did any of our usual things together – cinema, shopping, or just hanging out – the moment would always come. Sugar seemed to be the glue holding us together. He couldn't eat sweets while I wasn't because he felt guilty or ashamed or something. It wasn't OK for him that we weren't doing the same thing any more. I tried for a while.

One day, he was in a particularly bad mood. He often felt low and I saw it as my duty to throw myself into his sea of despair and fish him out. I knew that a cinnamon scroll from Brother Hubbard was his favourite thing to eat, so when he texted me in the morning and I got a sense of his sadness, I told him to shower, shave, get dressed and meet me on Capel Street.

I sat opposite Derick and ordered my coffee. He ordered his and his cinnamon scroll and then he looked at me. 'Are you really not going to eat something? Today!' He chose his tone to remind me that he was in crisis and I'd make the situation worse if I let him eat by himself. Out of guilt, and habit, I ordered the cinnamon scroll.

The cake arrived and the sprinkling of Demerara sugar on top turned my stomach. It wasn't that it was unsavoury: I felt sick because I knew that not holding this boundary was the wrong thing to do. Every taste bud was telling me not to eat it. My mouth was dry, which never happened when it was presented with a cake. I knew I had to hold my ground. Derick began to pull apart the sticky, warm pastry. Pieces of chopped walnut and brown clumps of delicious cinnamon tumbled onto my side of the table.

'I don't want this,' I said. 'I'm sorry. I'll get it to go and give it to—'

There was a silence you could have spread on a scone.

Derick continued to eat and took a sip of his coffee. He said nothing. I tried to change the subject. I dragged stilted conversation out of him, and after forty minutes we noticed there was a queue out of the door and the waiters were eyeing us to leave. We paid and left.

Outside the door I made a tentative plan to meet that weekend and go to see a show in the theatre festival. I left and walked home and, without sounding like the end of an Agatha Christie novel, I never heard from him again. I'm not joking. I've called, I've texted and I've sent Instagram messages. I know he wasn't in the happiest of places so I also know it's not my fault, and it wasn't just the cinnamon scroll. I can't help but think, though, that my starting to say no, starting to hold boundaries and have my own priorities had a part to play in the end of our friendship. It was as if Derick and I had grown into a mould. We fitted perfectly in our friendship exactly as it was. As I started to change and grow I no longer fitted it and the mould wouldn't change shape for the new version of me. I have seen Derick a few times since, around Dublin, and either he has blanked me or – I like to hope it's this option – he hasn't seen me.

I meet my mam every other weekend. She comes up to spend time with me and Nana. Sometimes the weekend she's in Dublin clashes with a commitment I already have. Not so long ago I had three consecutive weekends of being unavailable to see her. I picked up the phone. I had my story ready to explain but before I got even four words into the explanation she stopped me: 'Do what you need to do.' My saying no to seeing her was met with absolute understanding and respect. *That* is a powerful thing. Having a healthy boundary and honouring people's need to say no is probably the greatest gift you can give them.

Of course my mother could have guilted me into changing my plans and coming to see her. If that had happened I would likely have been resentful while I was there, which she would have picked up and felt guilty. Then, in turn, she would have felt resentful of me for causing her to feel bad, and the whole thing would have made for a toxic weekend in a caustic environment, and for what? So we could both say we had spent time together? No, thank you. Instead, when I did finally get the time to hang out with Mam and Nana it was a joy because we all knew we wanted to be there and no one was present out of obligation or fear.

People who love you accept that your choices and decisions are yours to make and are not a reflection or comment on them. If your friendship is built on a foundation of you saying yes at your expense, it's not a very healthy friendship and, while you might miss it terribly at first, one day you'll look back and see you're better off without it.

20

EVERYONE IN THE WORLD HAS EXPECTATIONS. IT'S PART of being human. People's expectations of us, however, are none of our business. Just because I *expect* you to offer to mind my dog when I complain about the price of kennels, it doesn't mean you have to meet that expectation. Just because your boss *expects* you to bring her a coffee when you go out to get one for yourself, it doesn't mean you have to get yourself into a twenty-euro-a-week habit. And yet expectations were one of the biggest hurdles I had to overcome once I started saying no. It's one thing to say no to an algorithim trying to get you to buy face cream, but it's quite another to say no to a historical, gendered and societal expectation of how you should live your life once you hit thirty.

Nowhere are expectations as thinly veiled as when extended families gather. These awful events bring out the worst in everyone's nearest and dearest. My own family isn't too bad. Of course, there are members who make inappropriate comments and embarrassing dance moves. Yes, I have relatives who make me grind my teeth down to nubs – I'm sure I raise their blood pressure too. But for all their dodgy dancing and shady one-liners dropped into the middle of perennial mealtimes, my family are not the worst. I realised how tolerable mine are at the family gathering of a guy I dated in my twenties.

Let's call the boyfriend-at-the-time David. I've never dated a David so that's safe.

David's family gathered in a hotel. As far as I'm aware, one of the oldest people left in the family was turning ninety-five and a child had to be christened, someone had got engaged and there might have been a university doctorate to celebrate, too. Whatever the accolades were, I know that they decided to have this massive get-together to kill all the birds with the one stone. And kill them they did.

I had two sparkling waters in my hands. It was a clever defence mechanism for me – it meant no one offered me a drink and I looked as though I was holding someone else's while they 'popped away for a second' so no one felt obligated to talk to me.

David has three sisters – Jane, Sarah and Marie, let's say.

At that party, Jane had been married for a year and Marie had just got engaged. Sarah was happily single. It seems that expectations are highly potent when it comes to other people's relationship status. The girls spent the day dodging expectation bullets in various passive-aggressive disguises.

'Sarah!' An elderly relative grabbed her shoulders and looked at each of them like a cartoon pirate checking the horizon. 'Still no man? Or is he hiding?' Sarah smiled without showing her teeth and glanced around for a way out. She was looking for someone to call her away, for the floor to swallow her, just anything. The octogenarian continued, 'If I hadn't seen all those posters of that Leonardo di Capricorn on your walls as a child, I'd think 'twas gay you were.'

'Marie! You're flying it above in Dublin in the bank. Your mother is so proud. 'Twould be more in your line to quit the bank now and give her some grandchildren.'

I made my way towards Jane but it was hard because her family had formed a solid mass, like the human barricade at the end of *Les Mis*. I arrived mid-conversation. It's less of a conversation, more like a bullet-free version of *Saving Private Ryan*. Verbal shots were being fired. I missed the opening salvos but I could see Jane was under enfilading fire from every side.

'Jane! You're not drinking. Oh, thank God, are you pregnant? We thought there was something wrong with you.'

'No, no.' She smiled and shrugged. 'I'm just waiting for the Prosecco to come back around.' On cue, the waiter with the Prosecco appeared and Jane downed one. The women tutted at each other.

'I told you, Mary, didn't I tell you? Didn't I say it? I said, "That's the weight of a newly wed. They let themselves go after the wedding always." I said it.'

'She did, Jane, she said it. I thought you were pregnant but Mary knew all along you weren't.'

I interjected as Jane downed another glass of Prosecco. Usually I don't get involved in other people's family dramas but I felt I would for ever after hear the sobs of Kitty Genovese if I did nothing. 'Jane, I've lost David and he has my phone. Would you call him?' Jane slid between the two marauders and came at me like a drowning child being pulled onto a lifeboat.

Not having kids is like the elephant in her womb. I think it's similar for many women her age. And mine. I remember when Kate Middleton and Prince William got married: every time she said no to a prawn sandwich or some awful cheesy offering at an event, the headlines would run riot with conjecture about her pregnancy. 'KATE EXPECTATIONS' was a running theme until the news broke one day that she actually was expecting. Then there was the detailed tracking of her bump, her pregnancy regime, how 'good' a pregnant woman she was, whether she was doing it right or being evil and eating shellfish.

Once she'd had her baby it was about how much weight she had to lose, how quickly she lost it, how she'd looked on her first public appearance just hours after the labour. It was insanity. And in that hotel garden at that family reunion, Jane was breathing in the fumes of all that hype in her own life.

I understand that convention is born of constant repetition.

It's like tradition or ritual. Society has survived and thrived because people have all followed similar paths. But just because 'it's tradition', it doesn't mean it's for everyone, and it doesn't mean it's right. There was a time when cannibalism was a tradition. That doesn't mean it still should be.

From very early on a sort of 'conventional lifecycle' is sold to us, even when we're children. Girls in particular are fed the following narrative:

You go to school.

You study hard and get good grades.

You go to college.

You meet someone.

You leave college and get a job.

If you didn't meet someone in college, now you meet someone.

You work and go on a few 'big' holidays to get photos of you and your S.O. on beaches.

On one of those beaches you get engaged.

You have a party for the engagement.

You organise a wedding.

You have a big white wedding with a chicken and fish option on the menu. (And a red meat option if you're really trying to impress Mammy's bridge friends.)

You get a mortgage together.

You buy a house together.

You have two cars in the driveway.

You have children.

You breastfeed them.

You go to work.

You pay your mortgage.

Your kids go to school.

You go on some nice holidays for photographs.

You retire.

You keep paying your mortgage.

Your kids have kids.

You spoil your grandkids.

You get old.

Your kids mind you.

You die.

You are buried in the ground.

Your kids fight over your will.

On it goes.

I set off on this travellator-to-the-grave just like any other Irish kid. But no one comments when you keep with convention. People only feel the need to comment when you break the mould. I put an egg white in my porridge. In my mind this is a vast improvement on the way people traditionally make porridge. Sometimes advancements and developments can improve people's lives. Now, with the egg white, my porridge doesn't give me heartburn. Is that not worth the slight deviation from what is considered 'normal'? Can you give me one example of how my porridge affects your life? Why do people get so upset when others choose to go off script when it comes to that long list above?

I broke from convention somewhere around number five.

There is an alternative conventional list for people who decide to go rogue and not 'get a job' right out of college. One of those *shoulds* is that

YOU SHOULD MOVE AWAY FROM IRELAND TO LONDON OR NEW YORK IF YOU ARE WORKING IN A CREATIVE INDUSTRY. AND IF YOU DON'T YOU OBVIOUSLY AREN'T VERY GOOD AT WHATEVER YOU DO.

I am still continuously asked, 'When are you moving over the Pond?' Sometimes they mean the Irish Sea and sometimes they mean the Atlantic. It's as if staying at home and forging my unconventional path is too weird for them and they'd rather I do my deviant stuff out of their sight.

It's important that more people stay here and push the boundaries of what is deemed 'possible' and 'right'. It's important to shake up the status quo to show other people that you *can* do things a different way. You can say no to the 'shoulds' and the expectations other people have about your life. These expectations can be gruelling for women. I have many friends who wish they had kids, but they can't. Others wish they could breastfeed but they can't. These are expectations of motherhood my friends had of themselves and they feel useless, bad and wrong because they can't meet them.

I don't know if I'll meet someone and have kids. That's not a priority for me right now. There are things I know for sure I'll be saying no to. I will not be having a big white wedding. I will not be inviting two hundred people to anything resembling a party. I will not hit my friends with a summons to an engagement party, a hen, baby showers, christenings and endless obligations to celebrate my life with me. And I will not be buried in the ground when it all goes belly up. I suspect we'll have run out of space by then anyway, and no one will be allowed to be buried. I want to be cremated and kept in a jar indoors where it's warm. Is that unconventional? Maybe. Is it OK? Definitely. And even if it's not, I won't know about it when it happens.

David's family's get-together day continued in its violently judgemental manner. It moved from marriage, babies, relationships and sexuality to something that seemed more innocent but actually wasn't. At one point, Jane's mother and a group of her friends were perched on high stools, watching the party unfold before them. Catching snippets of the conversation, I heard phrases like:

'That dress does nothing for her.'

'Wouldn't you think now she'd dress for her figure?'

'Sure people who are pear-shaped like that shouldn't wear stripes.'

'She'd have been better off in a dress. Those two pieces add to her.'

It was the kind of conversation that made me go to the bathroom and check myself in the mirror. It was the kind of conversation that, had I been wearing long sleeves, would have prompted me to pull them over my wrists and hide half of my hands. It was one of those 'chats' that make me feel totally insecure. The thing about opinions is that everyone has one. And, even though I tell myself not to care, everyone's is as valid as everyone else's. I try to remember that I, too, have loads of terrible opinions.

The Boy Housemate tells me the films I think are terrible are objectively *great* movies and that there is something wrong with me for thinking they're terrible. There is something freeing, I guess, in that we are all allowed to like different things. It's just activating when you hear people disapproving of someone's choice when it makes no difference to their lives. Their criticisms serve *only* to make the subject feel shit about themselves in the hope that the next time they're getting dressed they'll remember the comments and hang up their chosen dress in exchange for the Sarong of Compliance that was suggested to them.

WE HAVE TO SAY NO TO THE SARONG OF COMPLIANCE.

It's just as dangerous as the Kool-Aid of Conformity.

We don't need it. We have to say no.

I was overweight for the majority of my adult life. The only requirement I had of an outfit was that it fitted me.

People disapproved about my size in loud whispers, which I pretended not to hear. They sprinkled their advice all over me, like grated cheese on a pizza.

Things that were strongly or gently advised were:

I shouldn't wear tight garments or anything described as 'body con'.

The longer my cardigan was, the leaner I would appear (and that would be better for anyone looking on).

I should buy clothing that was designed and described as 'oversized' to help hide the 'bulk'.

I shouldn't draw attention to my problem area by adding necklaces that hung low or wearing belts on my widest part.

I should wear fringing to distract other people's eyes away from my body.

I should never 'tuck in' because 'tucking' draws attention to one's waist. I should avoid that at all costs.

It would be easier for me to hide my stomach if I layered my clothes.

I was consistently told that winter, as a season, was easier for my body type.

Oh, and, of course, this was often coupled with 'You have elegant hands.'

So my hands were the only aesthetically acceptable part of me. Was that it? Was I meant to cover myself in a sheet, like a nineties Halloween costume, and let only my hands show so as not to offend any onlooker?

I believed all of these things for two decades.

Each of the rules was of the same basic provenance. 'You are fat. Society will tolerate your fatness if you appear to be hiding it. If you have the audacity to wear a sleeveless top, we will let you know of our disapproval.'

I spent my twenties covered with shrouds and layers of loose material to hide my body from the world. I felt naked if I showed anything above my elbow or above my calf. My disobedient body was described as 'bulky', 'chubby', 'bulging'. 'Other people' referred to 'problem areas'. Who is it a problem for, though? I walked around with belts holding me together at my middle – I was like a Sellotaped pair of spectacles. Sometimes I thought I might actually fall apart if I took off that belt, if I took off the 'shoulds' and 'oughts' of how to be in my body. I measured necklaces, wore oversized handbags and bangles, made my hair bigger and my make-up louder. I did everything to distract other people's attention away from the problem. My body, The Problem.

I'm surprised I didn't burn more calories from the effort of trying to hide.

Then I lost the weight and guess what? THEY STILL COMMENT.

'You're too thin. You should tone your biceps. Tuck in your shirt to show off your hips. You have to buy long-length jeans – those are too short. You have a very long torso. That top looks cropped – get a different one. Your arms are too long for those sleeves. You look drawn in that necklace.'

WHAT DOES THAT EVEN MEAN? There's nothing more frustrating than a statement you know is meant to be insulting or pejorative but you don't understand it enough to be fully outraged.

I just wish I didn't care so much about what 'other people' think.

Rule: What 'other people' think is none of your business.

I mentioned that phrase earlier. It pops into my head regularly. I overheard an old woman say that to her ten-year-old grandchild on a train from Mallow to Dublin. So, shout-out to you if you're reading this. You got off the train in Kildare and I've never seen you again, but I hope your grandchild has remembered the advice as clearly as I have.

These 'other people' have more opinions than just how you're meant to dress for your body type. They're as varied and wide-reaching as daylight. Any decision you make in your life, there will be 'other people' to comment on it. If you choose not to shave your legs, someone's going to come at you with a razor or an eye-roll. If you join a gym, there'll be 'other people' to tell you you're wasting your money *and* 'other people' in the gym to tell you you're doing it wrong.* If you have a proper job with a pension, someone's going to ask why you don't go freelance and vice versa. It's endless. The mission is to say NO. Say, NO, NO, NO to other people's unsolicited commentary on your choices.

I ask for advice all the time. I *love* advice. But only from people I trust, whose opinion I respect. You can say no to things that other people expect you to do with your life. I nearly wrote 'You *should* say no to things that other people expect you to do with your life' – but then I'd have been hurling another expectation at you. And this isn't a self-help book so I won't say it. All I will say is shave your legs or don't. Wear a crop top or don't. Eat sugar or don't. Get a mortgage or don't.

*Doing it wrong at a gym can be quite dangerous. I always get someone to show me the rules and workings of the machines so I have someone to go crying to when I inevitably hurt myself.

To be honest, I really don't care what you do. I also know you care about me far less than my ego would like me to think. Let's make a commitment to each other. We can make it like a little wedding ceremony. These can be our vows:

*I, Stefanie Preissner, take thee reader
however you want to be.
Let's solemnly swear not to give a s**t about each other
in the most loving way possible
as long as we all shall live. xx*

Here are some other things you can say no to if you like:

I've left some blank so you can add your own.

1.   Moving to another country.

2.

3. Getting involved in any kind of hair removal.

4.

5.

6. Having a significant other.

7.

8. Going on an annual package holiday.

9.

10. Signing up to online banking.

11.

12.

13. Eating breakfast.

14. Waking up in the middle of the night to buy concert tickets.

15. Having a Facebook page.

16.

17. Being available.

18. Calling pizza a cheat meal.

21

IN MY TEENS, I WAS IN A COMPETITIVE SWIMMING CLUB in Mallow. We were called the Mallow Swans. The name sounds far more graceful than the fierce and often aggressive way we approached what most people would call a leisure activity. At the crack of dawn on weekday mornings we would get up and get dressed, get to the pool, get undressed again, then dive into freezing cold water. Our bodies full of melatonin, sleep still crusty in our eyes, we slingshot ourselves into the coldness to shock ourselves awake.

Swimming is a club sport but it is absolutely not a team

sport. Everyone in that pool was in it for themselves. As a swimmer I was never concerned with other swimmers. I had no rivals in other clubs — there was no nemesis I could target with negative energy and voodoo wishes of failure. The only person I had to beat at a swimming gala was myself. Each time a new race came up, the Stefanie of a few weeks previous was no longer good enough. She had to be beaten. Even if Stefanie of a few weeks previous had come first, or even won a gold medal at the goddamn Olympic Games, she was still not good enough now. Now there was a new race and the aim of every race was a PB. A Personal Best.

In swimming, you move up the ranks, graded A, B, C, based on your times for your event. Most of us started in C, then moved our way up by getting our 'B time' and then our 'A time'. Swimming pools are full of kids who can't tell you what they feel about bullying or what they'd save in a house fire but they *can* tell you – to the millisecond – how fast they can get through 200 metres freestyle. I knew swimming better than I knew myself. I quickly learned how to zone in and become hyper-focused on the tiny numbers on the stop watch. That made me lose all sight of the bigger picture. In that world a second was too long. When we talked about 'knocking four off it', we meant milliseconds. In karate there are coloured belts to show how advanced or novice you are. In swimming there is nothing external to show people your skill. You just carry it inside you. Your own personal best that could always be better.

I needed to knock 0.4 of a second off my time to get into the B grade. I had done it in training. The gala approached and I was sure I'd fuck it up. I'd fucked it up before. Queuing up for my race I walked past Francis, a ten-year-old swimming prodigy, who, people whispered, was 'bound for the Olympics'. I'd watched him swim earlier that day. He was already an A swimmer. He didn't have another grade to aim for. Once you got to A there were other tantalising demons, though. There were endless qualifying times for All-Irelands, Irish Opens, European Championships, Commonwealth Games, and it wasn't unheard-of for people to be aiming for the Olympics. Francis's eyes were bloodshot.

'Well done in your race.'

'Nah. My goggles leaked. I didn't place.'

'Did you get a PB?'

Francis started to cry.

'Francis, are you OK?'

'Yeah, my eyes are just sore from the chlorine.'

He walked away. I queued for my 100-metre race. I'm not going to drag you through the endless 1 minute, 23 seconds and 6 milliseconds it took me to get to the finish. I got out of the pool, asked the timekeeper if I could see the watch. There it was: my failure, in bold digits, for me to carry around until I could get rid of it by being better. I was 0.61 of a second slower than my best.

Striving for constant self-improvement is noble until it's psychotic. It's great to be curious about the world and want to learn new things. That's the impulse that makes us read and explore and develop. It gets tricky when self-improvement has no end-goal. When I wanted to learn kickboxing, I started out thinking I just wanted to acquire a skill, but once I was in there, the basics weren't enough.

Clearly, my swimming tendencies are still ingrained in me. Nothing is ever enough: there is always a better thing, a better way I could do it. There's always more I could achieve. This trait has pushed happiness to the horizon of perfection for me. Horizons are illusions. I'll never get to happiness because nothing will ever be perfect. Whole industries profit from our feeling that we can never be enough. The impossible standards we're expected to reach are crippling. Most often, I put such expectations on myself but they're influenced and informed by the media I consume, which is targeted directly at me.

The media is understandably polarised – vagueness and half-baked ideas don't sell magazines. People are much more likely to click, or purchase something with the headline '10 FAIL-SAFE CURES FOR ACNE' than '10 TREATMENTS FOR ACNE WHICH MAY WORK FOR SOME PEOPLE BUT NOT OTHERS'. The media we consume is directed, targeted and definitive. It promotes the best and the worst of everything, from people, to restaurants, to brands, to political parties, to music festivals – the list is endless. It makes sense then that we only see people at their best and their worst. We see people on red carpets having been in hair and make-up for twelve hours, then styled by a senior designer in some global fashion house. But all we see is the snapshot, the single moment where they're looking their best – or their worst, covered with vomit, falling out of a taxi.

The media love to watch us swimming in a culture of

scarcity, drowning in the feeling of 'not enough'. They can't cope with the idea that we might say no to perfectionism. Sure, even the section in which you probably found this book had some titles that were artistically rendered to make you feel like

(a) There was something wrong with you and

(b) They had the (only) solution.

There's nothing wrong with us, though. Not really. I've tried to be perfect and, because of that, I've seen minor shortcomings as massive personal failures.

I try to tell myself that good enough is good enough. I repeat, 'Done is better than perfect,' over and over. I'm trying to rewire my brain, to steer myself away from the need to be perfect and towards the light. But because I once said yes to perfectionism, it's a hard one to break. I'm trying to find a way to click Edit > Undo on the need to be right and good. I have to try to find joy in moments of achievement and not be already on to the next thing. I have to try to learn that done is better than perfect, that good enough is good enough.

I was 0.61 of a second slower than I wanted to be and it was an utter failure. I was saying yes to the impossible standards I had imposed on myself, or that had been imposed on me. When I write that sentence about the milliseconds I see how crazy it is. But another part of my brain has just said, 'I bet you'd be able to beat that time now. You're way fitter than you were as a teenager.' When will I learn, like?

The still small voice inside me, Little Stef, now asks me, Is OK enough? Can 'done' be better than 'perfect'? It's super-scary to accept that the things you do aren't perfect. Like this book. It's grand, like. It's not amazing or ground-breaking or life-shattering. It's not going to make Oprah's Top Whatever. It probably won't ever win anything that looks like a trophy but so fucking what?

20

WHEN PEOPLE SAY NO AS A GROUP, POWERFUL THINGS can happen.

The world is constantly changing. If you've read my first book, *Why Can't Everything Just Stay the Same?*, you'll be aware that I find change, especially big, irreversible change, overwhelming, scary and often catastrophic. As a global citizen, the changes in the world affect my life and how I exist. Another country's war, a change in president, a travel ban, a threat of nuclear war, an unstable economy in Europe, they all have a butterfly effect. Some changes are objectively better than others. For the greater good.

The other day I was in my favourite place to eat. It's a salad bar in Dublin city centre named Sprout & Co. It suits me to be able to choose from the bowls of ingredients what I want in my salad. I find in a pre-made salad there are always one or two things I'd rather leave out. This 'à la carte' way of eating has become the norm with me and my friends. I want the sweet potato and the chicken, but you can hold the rice and the red cabbage. This is a new way of eating for many people. Nana remembers when coleslaw came to Ireland. The idea of choosing each ingredient in your lunch is novel to her.

Modern Ireland strikes me as similar to this salad bar. It's an à la carte country that affords its citizens the dignity of choice. In my favourite salad bar, it's called a 'build your own'. Modern Ireland has looked at the menu we have been served for decades and said, 'No. No, thank you. We like some of the stuff – in fact we like most of it. The meaty protein stuff, like creating a social safety net, having a functioning representative democracy, an economy that grows at a steady pace, and a fluid constitution. All that stuff we'll keep. But there are garnishes and dressings we'd rather not have any more. We've learned that we don't have to accept the set menu. We can say no to three courses. We can have our cake for main course and we can eat it too.'

Not so long ago in Ireland you weren't allowed to be left-handed. Nana tells stories of *citógs* (a pejorative term for left-handed people) in primary school having their left hands tied behind them to force them to write with their right hands. That's in living history. I remember a time when you didn't have to stub out a cigarette if you were boarding a plane.

This country has changed considerably. Now you can be gay, straight, bisexual or trans; vegan, vegetarian, pescatarian or paleo; full-time, part-time, job-sharing or freelance. You can get the majority of your medical needs met here, and if you choose not to, that's OK, too.

If you live in the capital, (as I do: shout-out to Dublin 7) you can choose to travel to work by car, by bus, by Luas, by Dublin Bike, and if you choose to walk, there's a footpath all the way there.

You can travel abroad cheaply (or less cheaply if you want to bring more than 15 kgs).

It's à la carte living – build it however you like it.

You can have a spare room, or if you'd like to rent it and help out with an ongoing shortage, there's a tax break for that. And you can do all these things as *Gaeilge nó Béarla más maith leat*.

Imagine the uplift in national morale, the lightness and joy that was felt across the country in May 2015 and May 2018 when the power of democracy made itself known. When tens of thousands of people came back to this country for twenty-four hours to make sure it would be a place they could always proudly call 'Home'.

The current Irish government has twice filled the courtyard of Dublin Castle with people in tears of joy and hope for this great little country we live in. We voted yes: yes to equality and yes to repealing the eighth amendment. But every yes is a no to something else.

As a group, as a nation, we have said no to archaic views that promote and perpetuate inequality. We have said no to giving unquestioned divine power to the religious institutions that once governed us. We have said no to those who abuse power. We have said no to having our medical needs dismissed and outsourced to other countries. We have said no to being a generation of 'seen and not heard'.

I saw a video on social media during the marriage equality campaign. That movement mobilised young voters and moved some enough to register to vote when they had never voted before. The turnout at polling stations was well above average: 60.5 per cent of the Irish electorate made their way to the polls to vote on whether Ireland should legalise gay marriage. It was a higher percentage than the sixteen previous referenda polled, dating back to 1995 when Ireland voted to legalise divorce. What struck me as I stood in the long queue at my polling station was the number of young people I recognised as having come home to vote. A campaign had incentivised Irish people living in the UK to #gettheboattovote. Some ferry operators offered free or drastically reduced prices to help them travel home to cast their votes. It seemed like a gargantuan effort in which everyone rallied around. It was as though a whole forest of trees suddenly came to life and moved. I saw this video of a group on a ferry from the UK coming home to vote. They were singing 'She Moved Through The Fair'. The lyrics themselves are haunting and beautiful.

But set against the foggy backdrop of the Irish Sea, with the lights of Dublin Port coming into focus, I started to cry. I was sitting in some café with my laptop, crying at the power of what was happening. An entire forest of people was voting

YES but, equally, was saying no – no to the historical pattern of female oppression. I looked around the café at the people, none of whom had any idea that I was in the process of some kind of spiritual awakening. There were young teenagers.

I looked at one girl, who didn't resemble me in the slightest except that she had a Jansport bag and that was the brand of schoolbag I had when I was fifteen. I thought that if fifteen-year-old Stef could have witnessed this powerful video, this movement of young people who had been given (or had taken) their power, their agency, their control into their own hands and used it to stop the cycle of ill-treatment that had become 'tradition', maybe she would have learned earlier that saying no is a great and powerful thing. It doesn't mean you always have to say it, but knowing you're allowed to and that it will be respected is a powerful lesson for all of us.

23

WHAT PEOPLE SEE IS IMPORTANT. TERRIBLE THINGS become normal just because we keep seeing them. We become desensitised to tragic acts on the news; we think behaviours are normal because 'that's what happens'. Well, we can say no to what we accept as normal. Government leaders being racist is not normal. A woman being blamed for being raped because she was drunk is not normal. Children dying in inflatable boats as they flee their homes is not normal. Being able to see every single one of the ribs in someone's body is not normal. Drinking until you can't remember where your friends are is not normal. Having a relationship with someone where you never, ever disagree is not normal. Waking up in the morning with perfect hair is not normal – no matter how much the hair-spray commercial wants you to believe it is. It's difficult to get your head around, but you can say no.

24

I HATE-HATE-HATE-HATE-HATE WHEN PEOPLE SEND A text out of the blue saying, *What are you doing Thursday night?*

This text can mean only one thing. Someone wants you to do something and they're teasing you. Instead of just telling you what it is, being clear and open, they are reeling you into something that will be hard to get out of. I try to be honest in my life: it's the best policy. So I usually text back *Nothing* because usually I'm doing nothing at night. The response is *Great. I have this thing I want you to do for me/with me and I now know you have no excuse so it's hard to say no.*

Dear reader, please-please-please never send a text like that. No one appreciates it. Everyone gets fearful and anxious when they receive those texts. The initial text should have all the information the person needs to choose whether or not to say yes. It's not fair.

If someone in your life regularly entraps you into commitments in this way, you're in luck: I have found a response that has been working mightily for me.

Just as no is a sentence, nothing is an activity!

I now respond saying, *I said I was doing nothing. Nothing is an activity. I didn't say I was free.* I'd probably sprinkle that message with some emojis or extra syllables so I didn't sound like a bitch but they'd get the message.

Learning that I can decide what is important to me, that I can set my own priorities, is kind of scary to me. At least, it was at first. It felt so rebellious and anarchic to think that I could make watching *The X Factor* every Saturday night, from September to Christmas, my priority and not be available to anyone else during that time. If I could make such a guilty pleasure my priority, what else was I capable of?

25

IT WAS AFTER THE SHAKESPEARE IN THE PARK DEBACLE
that I realised I needed an agent, or at least some paid work.
Almost six months out of college, I was starving for work,
ravenous for the validation of someone saying, 'Yes, we
want you in our show above all these other people who have
applied.' I hadn't yet started to take writing seriously. It would
be a few months before I sat down to write my first play,
and in those months after leaving college I was desperate to
be seen, to be listened to, to feel like I was visible and that
I existed.

I sent my CV to anyone who would read it. I started with the big guns, which may hint at a level of hubris on my part. Below are some of the noes I got.

Hi Stefanie,
Many thanks for submitting your details to us and for the invite to your new play. Unfortunately I can't attend as I have a prior engagement.
  Best wishes with the production.
 Kind regards,
 Mr Letting Me Down Gently

Dear Actor,
Thank you for submitting your CV to the Casting Department.
  Please rest assured that your details will be kept on file for consideration for all suitable roles in future productions.
  The Casting Department
  A very big Irish theatre

Hi Stef,
Would LOVE to make it but I cant. Have workshops in Carlow!!!
  However, I will be thinking of you . . . with evertything [sic] crossed.
  Wishing you all the very best with it.
  Mr Genuinely Likeable

Note the font and misspelled name in this one:

Dear Stephanie [sic]
Thank you for attending our preliminary
auditions last Friday in Dublin. Our aim
for these early auditions was purely for
movement and voice/singing, while searching
for suitable actors to join our existing
Ensemble.

We have decided not to recall you for this
project but would like to thank you for your
energy and commitment on the day.

It is always a difficult process especially
for the actor attending – we hope you
enjoyed the process and wish you the best
in the future.

Thank you again.
Best wishes,
Mr Comic Sans

Dear Playwright

Thank you so much for submitting your play. We were

thrilled with the response to the call for submissions,

receiving over 1,700 plays which far exceeded

our expectations. We received plays about birth,

life, death, sex, love, loss, landscape, travel, grief,

climbing, falling, losing, winning, spirituality, carnality,

fishing and everything in between.

Unfortunately, your play has not been chosen to be part of the final production. Our selection was based not only on the standard of the plays (as the number of excellent plays received is far, far greater than the number we are able to produce) but also on the variety of theatrical approaches and the balance of subject matter explored.

In order to do justice to the level of creativity and interest that the project has generated among the Irish public, we intend to mount two separate productions — one production from 15-31 March and another production of a different play later in the year or at the start of 2013. However, as well as a small number of commissioned plays, this still means that we are only in a position to produce a little over 2% of those plays submitted.

Thanks again for your interest in this project. I am sorry that we are not able to pursue your play further with you on this occasion.

With best wishes,

Mr Detail

Those are just some of the many noes I got early on in my career. I get them all the time now but they don't sting with the same venom as the early ones. The early noes don't have any previous yeses to soften them. When all you have ever heard is no, no, no, you start to doubt that 'yes' is ever going to come. It takes a serious amount of intestinal fortitude to back yourself. It means saying no to how people make you feel about yourself. It means being kind to yourself when you feel like beating yourself up. It means rejecting and fighting the urge to look at yourself as a problem that needs to be fixed.

I had to accept these individual noes but I had to work really hard to frame them as minor. It would have been so easy, taken so much less mental energy, to see the noes as a no to who I was, what I wanted to do, my talents and my ability to make a career. It's as if I had to say no to the noes that were said to me. No, I am not going to let this rejection at work make me feel rejected as a whole person. No, I will not let this setback colour my view of myself. I may have failed but, no, I am not a failure. It is something I have, this rejection letter, not something I am. No, I will not let my old career guidance teacher be right.

When people say no to me – maybe everyone is the same – it makes me feel invalid. It's like I'm a debit card that's been put into a machine and, without warning, spat back out. You know that feeling? After the rejection, the questions start. What did I do wrong? Why don't they want me? Am I not good enough? What can I change, fix or improve to make myself turn into what they want? Even now when people say no to me I have to fight this initial instinct. I have to tell myself that maybe it's nothing to do with me.

In work, in relationships, if I'm honest and completely

myself, any rejections are now a sign of mere incompatibility and not a value judgement on my worth or contribution to the world. I can say no to my instinct to spiral into self-blame, reflection and criticism, and refuse to be drawn into the emotional chaos of finding an answer that doesn't exist – the answer to the question What Is Wrong With Me? Because, more often than sometimes, the answer is Nothing. If someone says no to working on a project with me I've learned that they're saying, 'No, I don't want to work on this project,' not 'No, I don't like you or feel you or your work is valuable.' Some days are easier than others, and sometimes maybe the person *doesn't* like me – but it never helps me to do other people's thinking for them.

26

AT THIS POINT IN MY REnoSSANCE I KNEW WHY I HAD TO say no. I had my lists and my criteria. I knew *what* I wanted to say no to. More often than not I knew *who* to say no to. I knew *where* I wanted to say no but *how* to say no was always a hurdle. It would be very simple to be able to say no as a full sentence. But life isn't simple and sometimes, professionally speaking, you want to say no to someone but you don't want them to hear it as rejection or disrespect: people are sensitive so working out how to say no was imperative.

When it came to work, I struggled just as much as I had in

my personal life. It took enormous effort at first not to give someone fifteen reasons why I was saying no, or why I couldn't do the thing they were asking me to do. I self-deprecated. I apologised for existing. I felt I had to defend my personality and position. It's still not easy for me to say no and leave it at that. Offering a lengthy explanation feels comforting, like penance. In fact, all it is doing is giving you an excuse to be resentful if the person is upset by your no. If I give a lengthy excuse – even if it's a lie – and someone comes back with a disappointed response or a counter-offer, I have reserved the right to be indignant. *How dare they?* Do they not understand that my fake cardiology appointment could be life-saving?

If you're thinking of shifting your life onto the no track, it might be fun to spend a week watching how other people do it. It can be quite entertaining to track the diluted, roundabout alternatives to saying no that have become socially acceptable. People generally know that you're telling a white lie because they've been on the same non-existent antibiotic to get out of whatever they didn't want to do.

In a strange way, those work noes I've heard throughout my career have taught me loads about how to say no to other people. If I set aside my ego, and my sophomoric response to rejection, I can pick out commonalities in the letters I received when I finished college.

1. They have made a 'policy' of their no to take the sting out of it.

We are only in a position to produce a little over 2% of those plays submitted and *The casting department will not respond to applications* mean that I don't receive the news as a personal attack. They're not saying, 'We will not respond to *your* email, Stefanie Preissner.' It's just policy and policy is never personal.

2. They use automated responses.

These can seem a little clinical but, like number 1, it stings a little less to remember that they have an automated response because so many people are being told no that personal emails are impossible. I think that was why the two where my name is spelled incorrectly stung that bit more: they valued me so little they didn't even care to spell my name correctly.

3. Fonts and emojis.

Getting a no in the Comic Sans font certainly helped to put the rejection into perspective. I doubt it was a conscious decision but when I received it I felt, well, did I *really* want to work for a company that sends professional emails in Comic Sans? Intentional or not, it took the sting out of it.

4. They sign off with their title/position/office rather than their name.

You can't see this in the text because I've omitted some details but these emails often come from 'The Casting Department' or 'The Head of Whatever' rather than from an actual person. This makes it easier for future encounters: neither of you has to dance around the shame of having said no or having been rejected.

I studied these rejections to see if they could help me to say no. After all, even though I had been told no several times by the same theatre company or casting department, I still came back. So, maybe if I said no in the right way, people would come back to me afterwards. From my own experience, using specific phrases and words to say no can soften the feeling of rejection and make declining the offer inoffensive because it's not personal.

I have parsed all the noes I have ever received and made a list of tools that help me when I have to say no. It turns out that some rejection letters are so expertly crafted that they register a very clear no but are not personal or cruel enough to stop me in my path and make me feel like a failure or an idiot for trying. The first thing I have to decide is how I want my no to come across. Sometimes people have been rude, outrageous or downright offensive in their requests so I don't try too hard to break it to them gently. Perhaps, in those circumstances, they didn't want me to say yes. Here are some of the things I've learned from the noes that didn't hurt as much as they might have. My tools can be applied in both personal and professional life, depending on your profession, I guess.

1. Add more vowels to appear less awkward.
This is often for a more informal setting. I have been told my tone in text/email can be 'officious'. I think that's a good thing, but the accusation was meant pejoratively so I've had to look at it. People often ask me things in text message, Twitter DM, or on Instagram. In these situations, and in some emails,

depending on the recipient, I find some extra vowels make the whole thing more friendly. I'm still saying no, and I still mean it, but it's dressed up in a non-threatening, friendly-polite costume. It might look like this:

Helloooooooo.
Great to hear from you. That sounds faaaaab!
Unfortunately I can't make it work this time but I wish you the very best with it.
Stef

2. Say it with emojis.

This is for when you have to say a fairly big no and the extra vowels just aren't going to cut it. Generally I keep my emojis in reserve for hard-core necessity. You can use the ubiquitous smiley face to appear more familiar and approving of the suggestion. I usually augment this with the monkey covering its face to indicate how frustrated I am at not being able to do whatever I'm being asked to do. Sometimes none of this is a lie. I'm often asked to do things I want to do but can't: the monkey emoji is perfect here. Please note: if you use emojis the person usually comes back and asks you the next time they want something so don't use them if you want to close the door to further requests.

3. Have an 'out of office' ready to go if you get there quick enough.

I can't talk this one up enough. It doesn't always work, but if the timing is right it's a Godsend. The biggest obstacles for me to saying no are my impulsive reactions coupled with my need to be liked. I feel like immediate agreement makes me a better person so that's the battle I have to fight each time a request comes in. Buying myself some time is the best investment ever! I have my emails on my phone and usually catch them pretty quickly when they come in, unless I'm in a meeting. If I catch it, I quickly copy and paste my 'auto-response' out-of-office and send it back to them. This is the most useful tool in my saying-no arsenal.

My out-of-office email says:

> Thanks for your email.
> I am away from my computer for a few days with limited access to email. I will respond promptly on my return. If your email is urgent please contact my publicist Aileen or my agent Jasmine. Their details are below.
> Stefanie Preissner

When something is requested of me, or someone makes me an offer, my natural instinct, from my schooling and upbringing, is to respond immediately. The out-of-office buys me time. So does this new practice I've been trying out in the last few months: I don't carry my day planner/ diary into meetings when I think someone may ask something of me. That way, I can say, 'Oh, shoot, I don't have my diary. Can I come back to you?' I also ask loads of questions and gather all the information I need before the offer is even on the table. It feels a bit awkward when someone asks you to do something and *then* you ask them about the fee or the duration because they'll know you're basing your decision on just those facts and – while it's often true – it leaves a weird capitalist pong in the air.

This leads me to number four.

4. Hire someone to say no for you.

Now, before you get annoyed and accuse me of having notions, hear me out. I'm fully aware that not everyone has the means or need to have someone to deal with the requests coming at them. I'm also aware that some people may have the need and the means, but having a personal assistant next to you at your desk in your accounting job might come across as a little extreme. So what can you do? Well, I have a friend who works in event management. He is a sole trader, an entrepreneur and a genius, but he is a one-man band. He realised that the business end of his business – the dirty money stuff – was tainting his relationships with his clients so he invented Dave. Dave is the fake employee of my friend. Now my friend can say, 'I'll have Dave from Accounts send you an invoice and follow up with you about payment.' Dave from Accounts is just an email address. Behind this simple technicality, my friend can be as officious about chasing payments as he likes, without any of it bleeding into his client relationships. Try it out. I can tell you that tooafraidtosaynotoyourface@gmail.com is taken.

Just the other day I had to get my publicist to say no for me. I haven't moved on too far from the days of getting Mam to forbid me to go to sleepovers so I didn't have to be the party-pooper. My publicist Aileen will often get a WhatsApp, saying, *John is going to call you to organise a shoot I have agreed to but I'm actually not able to do it. Can you fix my fuck-up please?*

Trying to figure out *what* to say no to can take a bit of mental work. I have to stop what I'm doing, find a hot drink and ask myself some questions.

- ⇉ Is this a priority?

- ⇉ Might I regret saying no to this in the future?

- ⇉ Do I owe this person a favour?

- ⇉ Does this person actually want me to say yes to this/do they care?

- ⇉ Am I going to have nightmares about this thing if I say yes?

- ⇉ Can I get a good photo out of it?

- ⇉ Am I being exploited?

- ⇉ Will it take me a step towards or away from where I want to be?

- ⇉ Am I hungry or tired?

The last is key for me. I can't make any good decisions in either of these states.

To add to my list of tools, I have put together a list of things I do beforehand to make sure I am in the best position to make a decision because – this is important – I might want to say yes to something because of my need to be liked. The following helped me to not fall into that trap:

1. Avoid in-person meetings where possible.

People will send an email with a nugget of information. I guess they think they're whetting your appetite. They will then ask to meet in person 'to discuss'. I have fallen for this too many times and would always leave having agreed to something I didn't want to do. It's hard because sometimes I really like the person and I want to meet them, but I know I can't because they'll reel me in and there'll be a massive clean-up.

2. Get all the info in writing first.

Knowledge is power in these situations. Especially timing knowledge. It's always lovely when someone gives you an easy out: I find that dates are my best friend. They tell you when it's on and, oops, I have a meeting in London that day. Sorry.

In my early days of using this tool I actually booked flights to be out of the country so I could put it on Twitter and Instagram and whoever it was would feel reassured that I hadn't lied to them. I have also been known to attach my boarding pass to things when it's a legitimate excuse, just so people don't feel duped.

3. Never be the first to sign up.

This one is crucial. If I don't know who's going to be at an event, I can't sign up. I wouldn't sleep in the run-up to it. The fear of the unknown gives me a worry pain in my stomach. In this case I ask them to come back to me closer to the time.

4. Make sure the person offering actually cares whether you say yes or no.

This is a HUGE one. Sometimes the person asking you doesn't care what your answer will be: they are only asking because they've been told to. When it's a friend or colleague, I assume they want a yes because they're asking. Figure out early on if this means something to the person asking, and if they don't care, neither should you.

When I incorporate some of the tools above into my life, things seems to flow much more easily. Life doesn't have to be a cycle of emailing another adult back and forth with 'sorry for the delayed response' until one of you dies because you're too scared of people not liking you. YOU CAN BE THE ONE TO PUT AN END TO IT.

You saying no will mean the job has to go to someone else, which may be an opportunity for them to develop their career, skills or be a bridesmaid. Your no can help other people to reach goals they've been aiming for.

27

IT'S MUCH SIMPLER TO SHIRK THE DEMANDS AND
expectations of your friends and family than it is to say no at
work. You can stand in a Wonder Woman pose, be 'true to
yourself', practise 'self-care' or just 'do you' as much as you
want with your nearest and dearest because there's a form of
negotiation in interpersonal relationships that doesn't exist
at work.

Most jobs come with a job description: a written list of
things you're bound to adhere to, things you must achieve,
processes which much be undertaken, etc. Your boss or

employer is allowed to have reasonable expectations of you if they're paying you for your time. If you hate what you're paid to do, getting another job might be the answer. For me, the problem arose when I loved my job – as it was written on paper – but couldn't tolerate all the other stuff that got Velcroed on to me as the weeks went by.

I was working, briefly, in a large company, with a team of other writers creating stories and plotlines for a TV show. At the time, it was my dream job. I was getting paid to write! I let go of any resentment I had that I hadn't been asked to audition for the show and prayed I wouldn't always have to speak about my acting career in the past tense.

It started out just mighty! The bosses made their values and expectations very clear. I felt confident I could meet their demands and deliver a consistent standard of work at our production meetings every Friday. I was happy with my bosses and they seemed happy with me. I had forgotten, however, after two years of being a lone ranger, touring my one-woman show, that it's colleagues who can be the most problematic aspect of a workplace.

The issues came like the tide, slowly at first, then all at once. The waves of one person's boldness crashed dangerously against the rocks of my politeness.

There was one writer on the team who continuously tried to fob his workload onto others. He was smart about it too. The request came hidden in a beautifully wrapped package of compliments. He would hand-deliver ornate prose, like 'I've been given the story line about the couple breaking their arms on the same day. But I read a piece you wrote about heartbreak and, wow, I was moved to tears. I think you could really bring something to that plot that I couldn't even come close to.' The fact that broken bones and broken hearts are utterly disconnected didn't register with me: the ardent flattery had me. He blindsided everyone with his praise and worship. The guy ended up wriggling his way into writing only the fluffy comic-relief story lines – they're the funniest, lowest stakes ones and can be a joy to play around with. He was lazy and manipulative and his work was not my job.

Once I cottoned on to his schtick, I was faced with a conundrum. I could confront his lazy arse and rat him out to the rest of the team to make them aware of his wily ways. But I also had to work side by side with him: being diplomatic was crucial. I decided to take a gentle approach. When he came at me the following Friday evening with the latest piece of work he didn't want to do, I apologised and sweated with equal enthusiasm. I gave him fifteen reasons why I couldn't do it, and a pint of perspiration. He backed away from me with his hands raised in a non-threatening gesture of retreat.

I watched him turn on his heel and make his way towards Mark. Two minutes later he was worshipping Mark. I've no doubt Mark spent the weekend slaving over two story lines while Mr Easy Pass wrote jokes on the back of napkins. He kept coming back to me with different forms of flattery. Some days I was ready for him. On others, I had worked out a new excuse because I could never say an outright no. Eventually I left the job because I couldn't do his work as well as mine, and the team aspect of writing just didn't suit me.

Sometimes I write at a desk in a shared workspace. I listen

to actual adults do actual jobs. They speak on the phone and 'do business' in a way that is totally alien to me. While I was writing this, I asked my publicist, 'Aileen, have you ever said no to a co-worker asking you to do their work for them?'

She said, 'Yes!' When I asked her how she had gone about it, she responded, 'I've just said I'm too busy with my own!'

I wasn't surprised. Aileen is efficient, direct, but radically kind. No one could take offence from her: they just respect her for being honest.

I tossed the question out to everyone in the room for a few more perspectives. One girl put in her headphones as a response. I guess not everyone appreciated my public interruption. Having asked the question, I found it fascinating that everyone had an answer. It seemed we'd all been taken for a ride at work. I texted a few pals to hear their thoughts.

One came back with *Just say fuckin' no and refuse to do what's not in your job description.* I read the message several times wondering how aggressive he'd meant it to sound. Then he texted again: *Want to go for coffee?*

I responded, *Aren't you at work?*

I quit. I'm on the lookout again. This guy has been asked to leave several jobs. His CV looks like the store directory of a shopping centre, the list of places he's worked is so long. I wouldn't take his advice on how to say no at work unless you want a way out of your job. An ill-mannered and ill-timed no will get you out of there quicker than you can say, 'That's not my job.' However, there is a way of getting to yes (the thing you want) through no (when no is diplomatic and considered) without losing your job.

From asking that question, and from my own limited experience, I gathered that:

→ Doing other people's work is something that should be nipped in the bud if it's looking like becoming a habit.

→ Helping someone out is not the same as being exploited by a lazy co-worker; as long as you are happy to do it and there's no resentment, it's all gravy.

→ Gently reminding someone that you have your own workload can work with most reasonable people.

→ For more brazen colleagues, a firmer no is needed. This can be scary and tough, but with anything short of a clear, uncomplicated, unexplained no, these weasels will find a way to talk you around.

I received one tip that I very much enjoyed. You send an email to four people. You make sure to include the difficult co-worker but the other three are plants – ideally friends who are aware that you are being exploited by the colleague. You tell the plants that they'll receive the email before you send it and assure them it is not intended for or directed at them. A group email allows you not to confront the offender directly. You can use sentences like 'Hey, guys, I'm really sorry but I cannot take on any more work that I currently have in my in-tray. Please do not ask me to do anything else for you. Thanks a miiiiill.' Add extra letters to appear less aggressive – that's still my favourite tip.

I've used this one myself with my friends. I was organising a dinner for a group of us (I organised it so I wouldn't feel bad about leaving early). One person hadn't paid and we all knew who it was so I sent a group WhatsApp to everyone saying I'd paid for two people and was sure whoever it was had just forgotten. All the others texted back immediately to say they'd paid, and eventually Ms Freeloader was guilted into coughing up.

My experience of saying no at work is fairly limited – remember when I was an actor and said yes to every role? You should be very cautious about taking work advice from me. I find saying no at work absolutely crippling because I'm afraid I'll be seen as entitled, arrogant, rude, proud or just not a team player. I've been working on it, though. I've been actively trying to make saying no easier by sticking to the rules in the previous chapter. I have become less impetuous (Jasmine, my agent, taught me that word and ascribed it to my business style) by making myself wait twenty-four hours before responding to requests. I have also sworn to the people I work with that I'll never agree anything over lunch or coffee or when they're not there. I just get so caught up in making the person in front of me like me that I'm liable to agree to anything.

We all want to appear helpful and polite but sometimes what is asked of you is impossible. Maybe you don't have enough time with all the projects you already have. Maybe you don't feel qualified for the role. Maybe someone else in the office would be better suited but they're great at saying no. Whatever the reason, saying no to your boss is sometimes crucial. A flat no or a passive-aggressive dance around the issue isn't going to end well. Whether we like it or not, the workplace may appear to be regulated and structured by HR and employment law, but it's really just a load of people and their personalities interacting with each other. Getting belligerent and highlighting the terms and conditions of your employment may keep you in a job because it's legal but it's not going to make for a very harmonious work week.

Having asked around, and from my experience, I've learned that a couple of things are key when you need to say no to your boss. The journalist Patrick Freyne gave me some solid advice on this one: sometimes you think a no is necessary but it may not be.

- ⇒ Figure out when a no is necessary. Sometimes bad ideas die on their own, but if you make the mistake of arguing vehemently against them others may become overly invested in them and put them on life support.

- ⇒ It would be a dream if no one had an ego or took business personally but they do so you have to speak to the human in the role rather than the role itself. 'Human pride' needs to be considered constantly.

- ⇒ A great way to say no is to suggest something different/better/preferable to you. 'No, but' or 'How about' can work wonders.

- ⇒ When it comes to more fundamental things – an ethical objection, a family engagement you can't miss, or you need time off because you're tired – give the reason, say no and stick by it. People who aren't nightmarish weapons will generally understand your no if it is presented in a calm, reasonable and well-considered way.

Maybe some of you reading this are bosses. If so, fair dues! But that role isn't without its problems. Terry Prone, chairman of the Communications Clinic, shares a couple of tips for delivering noes as a boss. First, be gentle and non-personal in saying no. Second, deliver little noes in a friendly way – 'Whoa. We don't do that, here. We never give backhanders. It's not moral and, anyway, we don't need to. Should have told you sooner . . .' This works, Terry says, because:

» It hammers home corporate rules.

» It indicates ethical background to those rules.

» It establishes a bit of pride.

» Importantly, the boss takes the blame for the misunderstanding.

I asked Mam for her thoughts on this one. She's a manager and has a lot of fabulous people working with her. She told me that sometimes an employee slips through the cracks in the interview process and it quickly becomes clear they're not suited to the job. The incompatibility usually becomes apparent when they start asking to swap shifts, leave early or have endless excuses as to why they're late. In every job some working hours or shifts are less onerous than others. If you're working in team, everyone shares the burden of the difficult shifts by taking one every now and again. There's always one person who dodges them, and they're always a source of resentment for their co-workers.

Mam said resentment is toxic in the workplace and leads to all sorts of bigger issues: you have to get rid of it at source as soon as possible. Employment law in Ireland is robust and just firing someone isn't the solution: Mam has to find ways of saying no to people in a way that makes them feel respected, but also highlights the ethos of the company so they can decide whether or not they want to stay there. She suggested never saying no and leaving it at that. Offer the employee some alternatives, like 'No, leaving early isn't an option today but maybe we can look at the rota with your list of doctor's appointments and see how we can make it work.' Or if the employee is looking to swap shifts, say, 'No, we don't swap shifts here, but why don't you email me your weekly availability each Sunday and I can make something work?' That usually leads to the person committing or quitting.

It looks like everyone has been shafted at some point in their life. In my tiny survey, it was clear that most of us have trouble saying no. I'm glad I asked other people about their policies around it: I feel less crippled by the fear of not being liked, knowing that others, maybe everyone, has felt that way. Maybe the only way to escape these fears is to change how we accept other people's noes. There's no point in everyone getting great at saying no if, at the same time, we continue to push people's boundaries and find new ways of getting to yes.

28

WHEN I WAS A CHILD, I WORKED OUT QUITE QUICKLY that sometimes no didn't always mean no. Sometimes no meant 'Maybe later' or 'I'm in a bad mood', or even 'I don't want to spoil you and I said yes already today', or perhaps 'Other parents will judge me for saying yes.' I knew from an early age that there were important variables when it came to getting what I wanted and I needed to box clever. I liked to think of it as a dance: the Choreography of Consent.

The first step of the choreography was delicate: choosing your battle. Parents of young children have a DYQ, a Daily Yes

Quota. You choose your battle, and you choose one you care enough to fight. Grown-ups can sniff out half-heartedness in a second. There are countless examples of me picking my battles but one sticks out as a recurring mission.

Mass.

On a Sunday my mother believed it was right and proper that, as Irish people who had been baptised and confirmed Roman Catholic, we went to Mass. My cousin's family was the same, although they often went to noon mass whereas we went at ten thirty, possibly to 'get it over with'. One Saturday night my cousin Sarah and I had a sleepover. We had stayed up late – like possibly even after 10 p.m. – and had got up early the following morning to eat Coco Pops and watch cartoons. Mass at ten thirty loomed over us, like homework on a Sunday night. My mam was still in bed at nine thirty so we thought if we were extra quiet she possibly wouldn't wake up and then we'd miss mass. The noon option was out because Mam was hosting Sunday lunch for Sarah's family and she had to be there to baste the lamb.

Sarah and I turned the TV all the way down so that we were basically lip-reading. We let our Coco Pops sit in the milk until they went soggy so the crunch wouldn't wake Mam. This was a Trojan group effort. We were on a mission. Nine fifty arrived and we heard movement upstairs. Disappointment showed in Sarah's eyes. I sat bolt upright and pointed my twisty straw spoon at her.

'No. We are not giving up. Not that easy.'

I convinced Sarah to give me a leg up. I climbed onto the radiator and pushed the clock forward thirty minutes. I knew my mother was too much of a perfectionist to walk into mass late. She'd rather be missing and have it assumed by the townsfolk that we were attending another service than march in late and be labelled a heathen.

Mam came downstairs, dressed for Mass. She looked at the two of us, suspicion in her eyes. 'Why are you two so quiet?'

'Auntie Bernie, we don't want to go to mass. Please can we skip it?'

She blew it! The whole subtle plan was blown out of the holy water because Sarah wanted to be honest. I was raging.

'No, we can't miss it. We *have* to go to Mass.'

When I casually enquired as to the roots of this rule I was told, bluntly: 'It's Sunday. You have to go to Mass on Sunday.'

Sarah started begging. Pleading. Whining. Whining is absolutely *not* a step in the Choreography of Consent.

I stepped in front of her. The data I have since gathered has taught me that presenting a calm, cogent argument that outlines the benefit for everyone involved, that doesn't come across as too much fun and, in this case, isn't overtly blasphemous is the best way to go. I offered a compromise. 'Mam, if we say the rosary in front of the holy-water bottle in the shape of Mary, then we don't have to get dressed and drive all the way to the church. That way, you won't miss the start of the Grand Prix and the dinner will be on time for when the others arrive.'

You know you've won in the seconds after you present your argument. If there is even a glimmer of hope, it comes in the form of a stillness. The pause is the adult considering your argument. If they say no after this it is simply a case of reshaping your offer or adding something to it. But where they're still, there's a way.

'No. No. We have to go to Mass.'

And because we'd had the stillness before the no, we knew we were in. From there it was about attrition. Just wearing her down, adding the offer of an angelus and an extra Our Father before the inevitable 'Oh, all right'. Sarah and I high-fived, thrilled with the win. There are few things as satisfying as convincing your parents to break the rules. Choreography complete.

We didn't end up saying the angelus or the rosary. We got distracted playing Nintendo. It all kicked off when we forgot to put back the clock and Mam missed the start of the Formula 1 race. We weren't blamed, though. I think Mam put it down to karma for not going to Mass.

Mass was one of the rules that had seemed like a law but became even less than a suggestion. At one time, in this country at least, you couldn't even dream of saying no to the Church. For my generation it's not like that: we've grown up being allowed to say no to all kinds of things that our parents and grandparents couldn't.

I had learned how to get around other people's noes. I had learned the jigs and reels in the Choreography of Consent – how to get others to say yes when they wanted to say no. If I was able to figure out this dance as a kid, imagine the complex tricks and manipulation a demanding and insistent adult could come up with, and I've been on the receiving end of someone not taking my no for an answer.

I don't like crowds. I don't like loud noises. I don't like being bumped into and I HATE ARCADE FIRE. Everything about the Arcade Fire gig in Dublin's 3 Arena set off alarm bells in me. I even hate arcades, and since my house burned down in 2012, I haven't been too fond of fires either. I said no. I said no about twenty times but Mr Selfless had bought a ticket *just for me* and I was being outright rude in saying no apparently. Don't you just hate it when people get you presents that are actually presents for them? Like 'Stefanie! Happy birthday! I got you this massaging mitt . . . you can't use it on your own back? Oh, well, I guess you'll just have to massage me then!'

Anyway, I didn't want to go but Mr Selfless knew that if he pressed my guilt buttons my inner people-pleaser would pop out and agree to be coerced into whatever he wanted.

We went to the concert. Mr Selfless is a massive Arcade Fire fan so we had to go early and stand right at the front. We were standing in 'the pit' three hours before the band were due to come on. One hour in and my legs were already hurting. I was bursting for the toilet but I couldn't leave in case 'we lose our spot'. That would have been the greatest blessing ever if it had actually materialised. Eventually, three hours in, hungry, weak from standing and with a full bladder, I summoned my energy to cover my ears when the bass kicked in for the opening song. I was being pushed, shoved and jostled by the heaving crowd. I made eye contact with a security man behind the barrier who took pity on me and mouthed, 'You OK?' I didn't think his capacity for lip-reading extended to 'No, I'm not OK. This guy next to me wouldn't take no for an answer and coerced me into coming to this concert and now I feel trapped and guilty and stupid and like I deserve every horrible minute of it.' So I nodded.

Towards the end of the concert one of the band members was leaping around the stage with some kind of portable drum, beating it like a crazed gorilla. He got so into it that he slammed the drumstick onto the skin and it bounced back and hit his forehead. Blood erupted from his eyebrow – it was like a ruptured fire hydrant. He continued to jump and bounce around with blood pumping from his head. I was horrified.

I stayed until the end, making a point of standing still, not clapping, not even looking directly at the stage. We were forced out of the venue with the mass of people leaving. The tram was full; there were no taxis or buses. We walked in silence along the tram lines. Mr Selfless decided to begin a debrief. He proceeded to recount the entire concert to me in real time, as though I hadn't just endured it live. I kept my head down – I hadn't the energy to lift it. At some point on the walk I noticed the drummer's blood all over my white Converse. I didn't know if it was from the Arcade Fire drummer or from my heart on my sleeve dripping blood onto my shoe. I felt a mild sort of violation. I had said no countless times and each time it was seen as another challenge, another step towards getting me to say yes.

I hated the media for reinforcing a Hollywood version of love in which wearing someone down is romantic. I felt angry with Mr Selfless, angry with the drummer for bleeding on me, angry with myself for not being stronger when I wanted to say no.

29

I WANTED A PARTICULAR WOMAN TO LAUNCH THIS book for me. I was having difficulty contacting her and was aware that just harassing her on Twitter wouldn't make me appear as the professional, respectful person I am. I asked a friend who works in the same circle as she does if he could connect us. He thought it was a great idea. He was all for it and seemed happy to help. I asked him to copy me in on the email that would connect us. The email arrived. It was perfect. Then I played it cool for twenty-five hours before I replied to them both, thanking him and introducing the notion to her.

Then I waited. After two days she responded. Agreeing she would be a good choice for the launch, and seeming excited about the concept, she said she had to check her diary and she'd be back to me.

Two weeks passed. No reply. I considered how long I should leave it before I gently nudged. I left it two weeks and two days. I sent another email. Nothing. Two more weeks and three more days, this time. Again, no response. That was four months ago.

I asked my friend if he would mention it to her again just to check what was going on. Maybe my email went to her spam folder or maybe the internet failed and I didn't receive her responses. My friend just said, 'No, Stefanie. She's already given you an answer.'

I got a little . . . indignant. 'Excuse me? She hasn't given me *any* answer. She's just being a massive unreliable flake.'

'There's no such thing as a flake,' he said. 'A flake is someone who felt they couldn't say no directly. Being flaky, or not responding, is a passive no.'

'What? That's ridiculous. She's a grown woman: she can say no.'

'She's Canadian. She's being polite. We call it a Canadian No. She doesn't like saying no, but that doesn't mean she's going to say yes. So she just won't respond.'

And that is how Céline Dion* came to not launch my book. She wanted my request to die of old age instead of having to tell me no. I'm lucky my friend was there to explain all this to me. I would have continued to email her, probably

---

* Céline Dion may not have been the Canadian I attempted to contact to launch my book.

getting more irate and sanctimonious about the fact that I was asking her to launch a book called *Can I Say No?* and she wasn't capable of giving me that answer. Then I might have posted her a signed copy, with the word 'no' highlighted every time it appears in the text.

Actually I might still do that.

30

MY FRIEND WAS VERY HELPFUL IN TEACHING ME THIS
lesson, in preserving my dignity with that woman and
increasing my word count with this anecdote.

We can assume that 'Céline Dion' didn't want the potentially
uncomfortable conversation in which she said no and I tried
to convince her. What did she think was going to happen if
she said no to me? I'm a joy! I'm non-threatening, friendly
and constantly feel like an imposter. If she'd said no to me I
would have responded with an email in which I apologised
in 2000 words for even asking in the first place. How could

someone be uncomfortable saying no to me? And yet when I have to say no I'm uncomfortable. In certain situations, I feel under pressure to say yes: I feel like my no won't be accepted or respected. I was making this woman feel as I have felt so many times – that she couldn't say no. Not accepting no, regardless of how it's conveyed, removes someone's autonomy and agency. It is stating that your request, or your need or agenda, is more important than they are. Feeling you can't say no is at best problematic and at worst traumatic.

When I started writing this book, I thought I had a fair idea what I was going to write. I thought it would be about people-pleasing – about trying to get Alison on the beach to like me, not telling Heather my ears weren't pierced, Rachel showing me that being kind to herself and saying no to me was a way of showing kindness to me, and learning that you have a right to say no. But I'm coming to realise now the connection between no and power. I was afraid to tell Heather that my ears weren't pierced because she had financial and career power over me. Rachel was afraid to say no to me because she felt I had the power and would break up our friendship. When I couldn't say no to doing Mr Easy Pass's work for him, it was because he had the power to make me seem a non-team player. It's all about power. Of course, I wasn't wielding power over Céline, but power and the word 'no' are connected. In short, it's dangerous when people don't take no for an answer.

When I find it hard to say no to someone, I'm worried that they might turn against me, fire me, break up with me, leave me, and if any of those things happened, I would be damaged. But what if I wasn't damaged? What if I took back the power and created a situation in which my saying no to someone is the same as saying 'hello' or 'table'. What if I reframed the whole thing? What if I reacted to 'no' in the same way that I react to 'tuna' or 'bagel' or 'ATM card'? It's close to lunchtime – can you tell?

I still find it uncomfortable to have to say no more than once. To mitigate the need for repetition, I try to be clear in my first no. I say what I mean and I don't say it meanly. Once I've said no I have to work on the anxiety that comes afterwards. I try to remember that once I say no, it's not my job to worry about how it will be received. It is my job to stick to 'no'. If people push me, I tell them clearly that I'm uncomfortable. It usually works.

Being tenacious is seen, by society, as valiant so you can't blame people for trying, but once you are very clear, you *can* blame people for pushing you. If it's a person in power, a boss, say, it's an abuse of their power if they press you once you've said no. This can be incredibly difficult because there may be very real consequences to refusing a request from someone in power. We are seeing the fallout of this across the globe with the #MeToo movement. Abuse of power is an epidemic and has to be stopped. There is no simple solution. There is no sentence I can put here, no tip or trick or hack, to guide anyone. The only thing I can say is that once you say no and it is not respected, you join an army of people who are fighting for change after similar experiences, and it is a battle that is not going away.

After 'Céline' didn't reply to my emails, however, I had another light-bulb moment.

'No' doesn't always look like no. It can look like 'not now', or 'I'm tired' or 'I don't want to' or 'I can't afford it' or 'Gluten makes me sick'. Or even 'Can I come back to you on that'?

Now when people say no to me – whatever form that no might take – I try to look at why they're saying no, and respecting their boundary, even if it feels uncomfortable or if I'm disappointed. Now, when people say no to me, I hear it.

31

THE CONCEPT OF NO AND POWER CONVERGE IN A perfect storm when it comes to sexual consent.

A few weeks ago I was going home from a press event and it was late. It wasn't midnight but it was well after rush-hour and I was on a commuter train. The carriage was empty. It wasn't 'almost empty', it was deserted. I remember because I took the opportunity of the empty carriage to make an Instagram story and speak aloud to my phone's front-facing camera – I would never have the nerve to do that in public.

The train stopped at a station four stops from mine. I put

away my phone and continued listening to Elizabeth Day's podcast. A man got on the train, looked up and down the carriage, then came and sat in the seat right next to me. It was a two-seater row so by sitting there he had fenced me in against the window. Of all the seats in the whole carriage he had decided that the one next to me had to be his. It was intimidating and threatening, like when you move your bishop in front of the other person's king and say, 'Checkmate.' I was trapped. All of the rules I'd learned at school came rushing back. None of the stranger-danger lessons but the less helpful ones:

>> Be good.

>> Be nice to everyone.

>> Share.

>> Be a good listener.

>> Don't make a fuss.

>> Don't cause a scene.

>> Be a team player.

I didn't want to cause a scene. I didn't want to be rude. I wanted the whole thing to be over. But at the same time all of the episodes of *CSI*, *Law and Order Special Victims Unit* and *Crimewatch* flashed through my head. I didn't want to be the next binge-worthy Netflix Original True Crime series. 'Can you sit somewhere else, please?' My blood rushed into my ears, my heart was pounding.

The man smelt like eggs and had eyes like a wolf. 'I want to sit here. You move.' I couldn't quite believe his audacity, his confidence or arrogance. If someone asked me to move I would be mortified and would move immediately. I didn't know what else to do. I stood up. Very quickly it became clear he wasn't going to move to let me out. Part of his plan was to force me to squeeze past him or climb over him. I wanted to scream or cry. I decided I didn't care about being polite. My confidence was reinforced by the fact that no one could see me. No one would be able to accuse me of being 'a bitch' or 'a weapon' or any of the other pejorative terms given to women who stick up for themselves. I kneed him, hard, in his thigh and forced my way out. I walked up the train, shaking, until I came across two teenage girls watching YouTube and sharing headphones in another carriage. I sat across from them, kept my eyes down and said nothing.

I called Rachel on the walk from the train to my house. I didn't tell her what had happened, I just wanted a distraction.

Was it rape? No. Was it sexual harassment? No. Did I get assaulted? No. But it was intimidating, traumatising and unnecessary. Instinctively, the guy knew he had a certain power over me. He was bigger than I was. I was alone in the carriage. It was late. He was in my personal space.

In the previous chapter, I talked about power and the word 'no'. It's especially dangerous when it comes to sexual consent.

Part of my brain sees consent as a matrix of complexity

and the other part sees it as a very simple two-letter word. No. But, then, I've been battling with that two-letter word for thirty years so it's obviously not simple just because it's a small word. We saw in the previous chapter that 'no' can look like all sorts of things – 'I'm tired' or 'I want to go home' or 'I'll call you' or 'I'm not feeling like it' or 'stop' and it can most definitely be non-verbal.

Because of movies and media, people think 'the chase' is a noble act. In business it's a first cousin of 'Make them an offer they can't refuse', and in your romantic or personal life it's 'Don't take no for an answer' or 'Chase the object of your affections'. To be clear, when I talk about consent I'm referring to heterosexual sex, and heterosexual rape, but the same applies across all genders and pairings: it's still about power. We need to remove the notion that 'no' will eventually lead to 'yes' if someone plays their cards right, or that the person you fancy is something to be conquered. 'No forced into yes' is still a strong message across the landscape of popular culture. This, alongside the popular trope that a woman 'chasing' the object of *her* desires is clingy or desperate, creates more problems.

I tried to keep my eyes and ears open for it as I was writing this chapter. Here are a handful of versions I came across.

I understand that pursuit is a key part of romance, particularly in fiction. We need to know how Jasmine comes around to loving the impoverished Aladdin. But there's a spectrum of pursuit, and actions can sit at one end or the other. They can be loving, generous and romantic or they can be creepy, stalkerish or downright criminal. Somewhere in between there's enthusiastic, over-enthusiastic and many others, which are sprinkled with honest good intent. I just find it bizarre that the tracking of women, unwanted attention and persistent invasion has become something to hope for in romance and is almost synonymous with men's passion.

Whether it's a man showing up at your house, uninvited, with a boom-box in *Say Anything*, or in *Scream 1*, Sidney's boyfriend breaking into her room at night because he wants her 'just that much', or Roger from *Sister, Sister* having to be told in *every episode* to go home, it's been reinforced in our psyche that this is romance. The Killers' 'Change Your Mind' is a catchy number I have found myself humming without ever listening to the lyrics or wondering what they're doing in the heads of people who catch them. The narratives of a culture, the things we see, the songs we hear, are important because they set up cultural norms.

It is not normal to make someone do something they do not want to do.

It is not normal to feel you have no choice in a compromising situation.

It is not normal to feel someone in power is abusing you and that you are powerless.

Normalising these behaviours is pervasive and dangerous and it has to be highlighted over and over.

Abuse of power is not just about sex. Power comes in many forms.

The #MeToo movement has been like the searchlight at the start of any Fox movie, or any episode of *The Simpsons*. It has started to shine a bright beam on the abuse of power, and the issue with sex and consent in the entertainment industry. It's been grotesquely enlightening but it has initiated many conversations in the workplace about how we might progress in a safer way and make sex and intimacy safer for the future. It's also sparked dialogue around workplace safety when it comes to bullying, mental health, harassment, power and the abuses associated with all of those.

Now I am ferociously annoyed by men asking, 'Do I have to ask permission before I compliment your hair?' or 'Am I allowed to shake your hand or is that an intimate touch?' Such bullshit is exhausting and tiresome, a roadblock to progress in sexual politics. *Obviously* if a compliment is paid in a genuine and friendly way, it will not be experienced as harassment. The fact that many people have an issue with asking for consent before they touch them, or ensuring someone is comfortable with their presence, betrays the crucial need for further progress in this area.

It's a journey we all have to make. But if we could go together it might be better than for some to race ahead, then chastise those who make slower progress. Worse still are those who decide not to make the journey because 'Back in my day the women were happier and there was none of this talk.'

I look back on my own life and remember incidents that I now see as problematic but didn't at the time. We know more now than we knew then. Even small things from the past I see in a new light. I was convinced by the trope of romantic pursuit as a teenager. It was probably from seeing Edward take the engine out of Bella's car in *Twilight* to stop her leaving, or from listening to 'Baby, It's Cold Outside' every Christmas and believing that a man going out of his way to drug you into staying with him was the height of festive cheer.

As I was navigating my way through my early crushes and

formulating my own romantic narratives, I unconsciously compared my puppy love to the stories I had seen or been told, and tried to mould myself into the shape of those stories. I tried to get boys to make me mixed tapes. I tried to get school yearbooks from the boys' school so I could draw hearts around the faces of the boys I liked. I would try to get ahead of a boy I liked in a crowd, at a swimming gala or on holidays because I believed I would be more attractive if he 'came across' me rather than if I approached him and started a conversation. I'd be gutted then when they walked past me and just smiled instead of saying something like Zack Morris would have said.

Maybe it was teenage insecurity, lack of self-esteem or hormones, or maybe it was me playing out the message I had received that girls who were passive, quiet and hung around, like decorative additions to a room, were more desirable.

Changing how young men are taught about masculinity and sex is a huge hurdle to overcome when it comes to the epidemic of consent we are seeing in the word 'no'. The motto seems to be 'Girls, say no, don't get assaulted', rather than 'Boys, don't have sex with someone who doesn't want to have sex with you.' 'Boys will be boys' needs to become 'Boys will be held accountable for their actions.'

I believe that if the paradigm could shift so it was a definitive 'Yes, please continue' or 'Yes, you may approach' and not a 'No, please stop what you're doing' the world would be a safer, happier place. When it comes to sex, it's not okay to proceed just because you haven't heard the word 'no'. Don't even start until you hear 'Yes.'

32

IT'S ALWAYS GOOD TO PRACTISE GRATITUDE OR TO take a minute to congratulate yourself on little wins. I learned this from Oprah. The goals you achieve should be marked. Here are some of my recent noes which I see as big achievements:

⇒ Doing an unpaid speaking event.

⇒ Granola.

⇒ The impulse to nap at 11 a.m.

→ Buying clothes in the Adidas online sale just because they sent me an email.

→ Being tricked into an argument with a colleague who was just itching for a fight.

→ Getting involved in *Love Island*.

→ Granola.

→ The spend-€50-get-€10-off deal that came free with my *Sunday Independent*. I don't need to spend €40 on groceries for €35 of it to be stale by Tuesday and thrown in the bin on Thursday.

→ My need to correct a typo in someone's tweet.

→ Granola.

→ The man who tried to get me to sign up to something in O'Connell Street.

→ The impulse to nap at 3 p.m.

→ The desire to stay up late watching reruns of *Friends*.

I feel like a kid who'd just finished singing 'The Itsy Bitsy Spider' with all of the associated hand gestures and is waiting for the adults in the room to applaud.

33

WE NEED TO TALK ABOUT GRANOLA.

Saying no to food is almost as hard as saying no to a child who's asking for a hug. To me they're basically the same thing. Food was a great friend of mine while I was growing up. Food taught me that I should never be uncomfortable and sad, and that if I ever was, I should just reach out to it for support and it would remove all the bad feelings. And it did, for a while. Humans are really bad at planning for the future. We are somehow hard-wired to prioritise our immediate satisfaction or comfort rather than projecting ahead, seeing our potential future needs and setting plans in place for them.

I am particularly terrible at it. I don't have a pension or anything resembling a rainy-day fund for my future. I am part of the #YOLO, treat yo-self, generation. We see self-care as an in-the-moment response to stressors rather than a sustained effort to mind ourselves over time. This is particularly clear when it comes to food. Saying no to it seems like the antithesis of self-care. When I want to eat granola, I WANT TO EAT GRANOLA. My body craves it, and saying no to a desire so powerful feels like deprivation. This is an important point but I feel like you're all going to hate me for saying it. So I'll say it really quickly.

Sometimes you have to say no to things you want in the moment to be able to say yes to things you want in the long run.

OK, I tried to say it quickly but I couldn't. Sorry.

I would never say no to granola. Its sweet, crunchy goodness is *always* something I want to shout yes at. I want to spit oat chunks out of my mouth while I scream, 'Yes!' between each mouthful. But by saying yes to granola *every time* I want it, I'm saying no to:

➤ My jeans.

➤ My other meals, which I will be too full to enjoy.

➤ My recommended daily calorie intake.

➤ My desire not to get diabetes.

As I write this, it's that awful dead time between Christmas Day and New Year's Day. It's a time when tiny expectations hang on the end of every sentence. There are more opportunities to be a yes-woman than there are twinkly lights on my mother's Christmas tree. (My mother has to pay her December electricity bill in instalments.) The silly season has a thread of self-sacrifice woven into it. It's the season of giving.

This would be fine if there was a caveat clause that said, ''Tis the season of giving . . . as much as you can but no more.' Economists are rolled out to comment on the amount of money that is spent in the run-up to Christmas. Shops complain that they are losing money because people are getting better deals online. It's a festival of frivolity where we all get the chance to tell our nearest and dearest we love them 'this many bucks' worth'. If you really want to hammer home the message, you leave the price tag on just in case the gift is small and the recipient equates its size with its price. God forbid someone would think you only love them four inches' worth when the four-inch gift cost a hundred euro. It's a draining, competitive, fraught and highly charged time of year when everyone gets the same props and costumes because many of us have similar traditions around Christmas – turkey, Christmas movies, charades, sequins, mulled alcohol and excess sugar. It's the perfect time of year to compare yourself to the TV commercials, Christmas card photos and Hollywood versions of Christmas. We are walnuts smashed open by a nutcracker, veins bulging and stomach acid crawling up our throats with the effort of trying to have *the perfect Christmas*.

It's like a Beckettian torture, this impossible task we undertake every twelve months. If you try to say no to the endless expectations you end up being called Ebenezer Scrooge or having some other Dickensian insult like 'Humbug!' hurled at you, followed swiftly by a mince pie to the face.

I have yet to succeed in saying no to the expectations of Christmas. December rolls around and the snow globe inside me gets all shaken up and I find myself swept away in the mayhem. It concludes with tears on Christmas Day, usually silent, non-dramatic tears in a bathroom. I usually cry because Christmas Day isn't what I imagined. It's ridiculous because every Christmas Day is the same, but every year I align my expectations to the mass-media myths of what Christmas *should* be. It's a no I'll continue to work on saying.

However, there's one festive no that rears its ugly head every year, usually around 28 December, and I have managed, *finally*, to say no to it. It came up on my Instagram feed again today (29 December) and I was so enraged I had to write this.

Just as the world puts Michael Bublé back in his bubble wrap, thanking him for providing another year of background music to millions of festive gatherings, there is a different, sinister beast stirring. He waits until Bublé and Mariah sing their final notes, then comes at us.

The 'Be Better Beast' is a billion-dollar industry. He comes into our phones and our homes before we've even digested our last roast potato to make us feel shit about whatever joy we've experienced in the previous few weeks. The Be Better Beast needs you not to get comfortable with the idea of being relaxed, of eating what you want, of accepting gratuitous love, of lying on the couch and watching movies with no guilt. The Be Better Beast is terrified that you might actually find some serenity and self-love if you were left in Christmas mode for too long. He huffs and he puffs and he blows your self-esteem down.

Post-Christmas guilt is getting more problematic every year. Diet culture and messages reinforce the concept that you are more valuable the smaller you are: they are dangerous and pervasive. It's not just size and food, but there is a lot of that in how the Be Better Beast operates. His basic message is just Be Better. Which is another way of saying . . . you're not good enough. The foundation of this industry is based on making you feel that after Christmas you can 'redeem' your bad self and that you are better the more restricted your diet is, the more often you are in the gym, the heavier the weights you lift, the more you sweat and the less you enjoy January. It's worth noting that January is associated with being the most depressing month of the year. I can't help but draw a link here. It's easier to feel shit when a whole industry is trying to make it so.

Watch out for it and know that you can say no. I now say a big fat no to the Be Better Beast. I make a point of doing the exact same things on St Stephen's Day and the following few weeks. I don't join a gym, buy new active-wear, change my diet, or any of that scary bullshit. I unfollow any Instagram accounts that spin the 'New Year New You' stuff. I unsubscribe from any site that emails me a January discount for anything even vaguely to do with self-improvement.

It's sort of fun since I've changed my outlook. Now I see it almost as a game. I get disappointed in my local health-food shop when they try to make me buy a new supplement that guarantees to 'rejuvenate' my liver after my Christmas 'binge'. I laugh and click 'unfollow' when some brain-dead influencer starts telling me about 'adrenal fatigue' in a post littered with typos alongside scaremongering exclamation marks. It's a time when the only thing that gets more exercise is my bullshit filter, and my eyeballs from being on the lookout for traps to make me feel shit.

I started saying no to the Be Better Beast a few years ago and I haven't looked back. It's money-making madness that profits on your insecurities and self-doubt. Your body is well able to get rid of toxins by itself – have you ever eaten something that's gone off and been on the toilet all night? You don't need to do a detox and you *certainly* don't need to pay to do one. Give yourself a break and say *no* to this. If you can't say no just yet, start to become curious about the language you see around Christmas and New Year, and ask yourself if that person/account/business could stand to make a profit from you believing what they're saying.

Food is a powerful thing. It's cunning and baffling, and it calls out to us in times of insecurity and uncertainty. If I feel a bit guilty for saying no to a friend or at work, I find saying no to food *really* hard. It's just there, waiting to wrap a blanket around the guilt in my stomach. It layers itself on top of the uncomfortable feelings so I don't notice them. But then summer comes, or maybe even the weekend, or later that same day, and I don't just feel bad for saying no to work or my friend or whatever it was, I now also feel bad for eating a whole packet of granola. There is no need to add to the list of things you feel guilty about. Either eat the granola and leave out the guilt or don't eat the granola. I tried the former and it didn't work so I just don't buy the granola. I only have so much willpower in a day.

It's the guilt that's the real issue. What if you had never heard a value being put on food? What if treats and cheat meals just weren't a thing? What if we ate what we wanted, when we wanted and hadn't been socialised out of our bodies? What if we could still trust our guts on more things than just spam emails looking for our bank-account details? Sometimes my body craves sugar. It happens around the same time each month, and each month I inevitably feel like there is something wrong with me. I have read so many 'sugar-free" books. I have bought, photocopied and downloaded more graphs and manuals on how to be healthy and how to quit sugar than I care to admit.

The result, apart from my drastic cutting-down on fructose, has been that I feel like a bad person when I crave sugar, like there is something deviant about my desire. It feels like a dirty, bad, negative want that belongs under a bridge and hidden in the dark. It makes me so hard on myself and go to such lengths to avoid it that I often end up obsessing about sugar. All that guilt is learned. I wish I could say no to it instead of draining myself with the effort that takes. Surely there's no need to feel guilty about giving your body what it craves when it's really craving it. Surely not making myself feel like a monster would be better.

I'm still figuring this one out. I want to say no to being 'good' when it comes to food and body. I want 'being good' to look like kindness, empathy and loyalty. I don't want any virtue attributed to me when I say, 'I don't eat sugar.' I don't want people to congratulate me because I've lost weight as though I'm inherently a better person than I was beforehand. I want to say no to the discourse and language around food and body. I want people to accept that bodies and food habits differ from person to person, and if something's not having a negative impact on your health, then what is the problem?

Sure, if you want to, say no to the cake, but don't say no to it because you believe your no is making you more worthy of love or acceptance in the world.

34

I'VE SAID NO TO COUNTLESS WEDDINGS. I THINK weddings are sort of ridiculous. I wonder if someone proposed to me would I still feel the same. It's as though weddings operate on the fact that people are afraid to say no. The happy couple invite 300 people when they know the venue only seats 250. They *expect* people to say no, but there's always this panic when more than 250 say yes – often out of obligation and just because they've been asked: they feel too guilty to say no. Everyone knows people invite extra but they never think *they* are the extra people whom the bride is hoping will decline to attend. It's that thing I was talking about before, of taking no for an answer. If we only invited who we wanted, everyone would know they were wanted and they wouldn't have to ask themselves, 'Does she want me to come or am I one of the extra people who is only invited to up the haul of presents?' The social pressure to invite everyone you've ever met, coupled with the social pressure to RSVP yes to everything you're ever invited to, has made plenty of about-to-be-weds panic-order more wine and turn six-seater tables swiftly into eights.

Have you ever wondered why you only get two small slices of turkey at those wedding dinners? Well, it was meant to be three but everyone said yes, and then there wasn't enough to go around.

Getting married on a picturesque European island is the latest racket. I blame Pinterest. As if weddings weren't enough of an investment already for guests, now they have to invest more time as well as more money. Michael O'Leary, who owns Ryanair, is laughing all the way to the bank. People who get married abroad usually have a teacher in their close family or kids are involved as flower girls or confetti-throwers. This means that the wedding has to take place during mid-term, Easter or summer holidays, which in turn means that the price of flights is *waaaaay* higher than if they got married on a random Thursday in November.

Ryanair is usually the cheapest airline when it comes to those island airports but they don't offer daily flights. The schedule means a diminished chance of popping over the day before the wedding, taking a few choice Instagram pictures, dancing to 'Come On Eileen' and 'Rock The Boat', then popping home, hungover, the following day. You're probably going to have to fly in on a Tuesday at, like, 4 a.m., then the next flight will most likely be the day of the wedding so you're stuck for a week, with all the extra hotel nights that that entails. Also, because of the sheer number of people flocking to the tiny beach resort (chosen for its flower walls and white sand beaches), there's probably a hike in hotel-room prices, if you can get one at all.

Worst-case scenario: you book your flight only to find there's no room available and you have to bunk in with bachelor Billy, who attends everything and has booked a double room for precisely this reason. You arrive into his hotel room with your 15-kg suitcase. He winks and says, 'Every wedding leads to another.' Wiggling his eyebrows, he closes the door. *Shudder.*

The plus side is that this kind of a wedding usually provides guests with flip-flops for the dance floor and sweets with the bride and groom's initials printed on them. The expiry date on the sweets may outlast the marriage. Hopefully not, though. I sound like such a bitch. I do wish all of my married friends long, long happy lives together. But if you do get divorced, try to remarry someone with the same initials so you can reuse all the personalised party favours you got for the first wedding. S&R branded dessertspoons are always in, right?

35

WHILE IRELAND WAS SAYING NO TO THE PARTS OF ITS
menu that felt a little stale, people in other countries were
saying no too. But for every no there's always an equal and
opposite yes.

It's sort of impossible to write about this because the facts
change as fast as stocks and shares. Actually, the changing facts
are the cause of the fluctuation in the global market economy.

In 2016 it seemed like everyone had just had enough. All
the systems that had been moving along for decades just came
to a halt. Brangelina said no to each other. Apple Inc. said no

to headphone jacks. Democrats said no to Bernie Sanders. The USA voted for Trump and, regardless of our political leanings, I think we can all agree the whole process was harrowing and awful. And life said no to a series of heroes including Harper Lee, Muhammad Ali, Gene Wilder, Carrie Fisher, Debbie Reynolds, Prince, David Bowie, George Michael, Alan Rickman, and too many others. Harambe the Gorilla was killed in Cincinnati Zoo for checking on a kid who fell into his cage. Immune systems struggled to say no to Zika and Ebola as they raged across the globe. Someone said no to continuing production of the TV show *House of Lies*, a personal favourite.

2016 was for the world what 2007 was for Britney Spears.

Saying no as a society can lead to great change. Great change can be constructive or chaotic. Perhaps it depends on your perspective. One person's yes is another person's no. In 2015 I felt elated when the marriage-equality referendum resulted in Yes. I felt equally satisfied with the liberal and progressive direction in which Ireland was moving when we voted on the eighth amendment to our constitution and legalised abortion. I was horrified in 2016 when Brexit happened and Trump was elected. However, if we assume these elections were above board and all voting was honest and democratic, the majority were not horrified. For every glass downed in sorrow, another was raised in celebration.

I was in the USA when Trump was elected. I expected everyone to be as shocked as I was at the news. But there was no shock or outrage in Dallas, Texas, where I was working. I was, for the first time in ages, in the minority.

It was baffling, but the hope in Texas was contagious and almost palpable. It was an audacious, gun-carrying kind of hope for the future, and for change by people who had merely tolerated Obama. There was a real sense of 'Y'all had your turn at hope. Now it's ours.'

The snippets I caught at the gas station or at the rodeo were like the soundbites I heard on the streets of Dublin in May 2015, the day after Ireland voted yes to marriage equality. Public morale seemed high in Texas. A colleague had travelled with me from New York: he was withered by the result. On seeing the celebrations around us he asked, 'Is what I'm feeling now how the racists felt when Obama was elected?'

I think there's something to be learned from the changing politics of the world and until we learn it we're never going to have peace. I don't even mean world peace, even just peace of mind, I mean a piece of peace in your own head. Different people want different things. One person's Yes is another person's No. And crucially, if you want to live in a democratic society you have to accept the majority rule, even when it doesn't go your way. You may feel like an outsider within your own tribe.

It's difficult to let something go once you've campaigned and voted for it. It requires mammoth levels of magnanimity to accept that the majority wants something you don't, especially if you think dishonesty has been at work. With Cambridge Analytica, Russian meddling and all the lies, fake news and click bait that get churned out during elections and referenda these days, it's hard to accept that most people would have a different opinion from me.

No, sorry, I meant 'It's hard to accept that the majority of people *wouldn't* have a different opinion from me.' It's a double-negative kinda thing as Donald Trump would say.

36

SO IT'S ALL GOING SWIMMINGLY. I HAVE MY PRIMARY
purpose and I ardently say no to anything that distracts from
it. Then one day I'm at my laptop, typing away, and Nana
rings. She wants to know if I'll pick her up some croutons
and milk if I'm passing a shop because she isn't feeling up to
going out today.

Shit. Maybe I haven't thought this through.

I hate saying no to Nana. When she's gone I don't want my
memories of her to be a list of things I said no to. I want my
loved ones to feel they're always a priority to me. This is tricky

and I don't always get it right. I put Nana's appointments in my diary before anything else. If I'm scheduled to take her to her cardiologist or her optometrist, it takes precedence over any meeting I might have. If it's in the diary, it's set in stone. It's easy to say yes because it's something I want to do. But I tend to structure my life around work, deadlines and being productive. If I'm not careful I can forget to leave space for family, friends and contingency. So when things pop up I'm not in a place to say yes when I want to. There's nothing worse than having to say no when you want to say yes. Avoid, avoid, avoid.

Is it OK to change my primary purpose to being a good granddaughter? What's the priority here?

37

ONE WEEK RECENTLY I RECEIVED TWO INVITATIONS.

1. To go to a Taylor Swift concert with friends.

2. To have lunch with a friend I see quite often.

I had a deadline for this book and needed to get 5,000 words written over the weekend: 2,500 words a day. The 'place I wanted to be' was having a finished book and, because that's my job, that was my priority. I worked out that I didn't know very many Taylor Swift songs and I don't like concerts so my immediate response to invitation no.1 was no. But I held off giving that answer and I talked to the friend who had offered the ticket. I needed to figure out how much it meant to her that I was there.

'Pal, would you like me to go to the concert with you?'

'Ya, sure, come along if you want, it'll be the craic, like.'

'But do *you* want me to go?'

'If you want to come, of course.'

This is where it gets tricky. My friend wanted me to feel welcome: she felt uncomfortable saying, 'I don't care if you come or not,' because she wanted me to feel I was wanted. So I had to rephrase.

'Pal, I don't really have that much interest in a Taylor Swift concert. But I'd love to do it if it meant something to you.'

'Oh, no, I don't care, like. I just have an extra ticket.'

Grand. I said no and she didn't mind in the slightest. I later found out that she'd sold the ticket at the entrance so she was thrilled I didn't take it.

The lunch invitation was slightly different. My friend knows I have a routine when it comes to meals. I'm tortured by my lack of capacity to relinquish control. *I'm sorry I'm a control freak. I'm really trying to stop.* I like to know where I'm eating and I eat at the same times every day. She was planning to go hiking before lunch on Saturday and wasn't sure what time she'd be back down the mountain or what food she'd want. This was all too nebulous for me so I had to say no. Now, I see this friend a lot so I didn't feel too bad. If it had been a friend who was looking to catch up I would have made more of an effort to build my day around hers. But I had my deadline, which was the priority, so I kept my day clear.

Saturday arrives. I wake up before the world does. It's just me and the white-hot sun at 4.45 a.m. It calls me towards the kitchen: 4.45 a.m. goes best with coffee.

I boil the kettle and close my eyes as it bubbles. I wonder if it's possible to get sunburned through double-glazed windows and a Venetian blind. It's July 2018 and Ireland is officially experiencing a drought. It's not even 5 a.m. and my phone is telling me it's 21 degrees centigrade.

The kettle clicks and I start what other people would disregard as a meditation. The routine and ritual around how I make my first coffee of the day is meditative.

When I make coffee, I can turn off my mind for a few minutes. I don't have to worry about all the things I worry about. I put the filter into my coffee-maker and pour in the Colombian roast. That sounds *waaaay* posher than it actually is. I get my coffee from Tesco, its own brand coffee. I like the shiny purple packet. I carefully measure two scoops with the little plastic thingy that came with my coffee-maker. I make sure not even one brown grain drops onto the white surface of my kitchen counter. I pour the just-boiled water over the coffee and the steam of it, the smell of it, wafts up to welcome me to Saturday. The sun in my face, the smell in my nostrils, the feel of the steam hitting my chin and face . . . I breathe it in.

In for three.

Hold for four.

Out for three.

Sure it's basically yoga at this point.

The smell of the coffee dissolves the worries. For the few brewing minutes, I watch the water trickle through the coffee until all that's left is something that looks like mud in the filter. For those few minutes the water drips into the cup, filling it slowly, and the worries drip out of me, keeping pace. I'm not thinking about deadlines or word counts or when Nana is going to die. I'm not trying to time a break from writing so I can call the bank, my accountant, my recycling provider and Bryan-who's-coming-to-put-up-shelves in a ten-minute window. I just make the coffee. There's a silence you could spread on toast. But it's not breakfast time yet. It's possibly the only thing I do that I can keep simple.

I take my coffee, turn my back to the sun and the kettle. I have a sip to propel me back up the stairs and I'm at my desk, writing, by 5 a.m., my brain whirring like an old diesel engine again, polluting my environment with dangerous toxins, dangerous fictitious thoughts.

I get great joy from sitting alone, writing. There's a particular strain of this joy when I know I don't have to be anywhere at 9 a.m. If I have only two hours to write, I'll get it written for sure. But the time constraint places an extra dimension of pressure on the task. It's like if you took the ticking clock away from the thirty seconds on *Countdown*: it would be much calmer and they'd likely come to the same words in the same amount of time. The clock is just there to add dramatic tension.

It's Saturday and I have nothing planned except writing. The Boy Housemate is away for the weekend so it's just me. I've said no to lunch with a friend because she couldn't commit to where to go and I like to have a plan. Everyone else is going to watch Taylor Swift singing songs at them. I've said my noes and the day is mine.

At 8 a.m. I break for breakfast. It's one of those mornings where I'm in the flow. Creativity or some unidentified muse has lubricated the gap between me and my thoughts. Words flow from my fingertips into my MacBook and all of a sudden my Apple Watch is reminding me that I haven't stood for three full hours. (Oh, yeah, I fully drank Steve Jobs's Kool-Aid. I am a total conformist when it comes to Apple products. I like not having to sacrifice aesthetics at the altar of utility. I even use Safari as my browser. Sorry if that offends anyone.) I've written about 3,500 words and my quota for the whole day was only 3,000. I feel good!

I make my breakfast. I like to eat the same 'porridge with benefits' each day. I call it 'augmented porridge'. It's a secret recipe that involves the egg white I mentioned earlier and that's all I'm saying. I turn on the radio in the background. The station is playing Kanye West's 'Runaway' and the start of the song sounds like the microwave complaining at me. I get lost in thought while the radiation softens my oats. Now that I've done all the writing I need to do, how will I spend the day?

I eat my porridge with this question still whirring around. I text my friend who wanted to meet for lunch to see if me suggesting a location will appeal to her now. She responds immediately even though it's 8 a.m. She's just getting in from an impromptu night out and she'll text me when she wakes. That's a no. I text a few others. They're all sleeping late or having a lazy day to preserve their energy for later. How much energy can it take to watch someone singing? When they offered me a ticket to go with them, they made it seem like it was going to be fairly laid-back. Why are they acting like snakes in the desert now, lying on a rock in the shade to conserve their store of energy from the sun? I consider visiting Nana, but a pang of guilt makes me almost choke on one of my porridge blueberries. I don't want to visit Nana just because I have nothing else to do. That's what shopping is for.

I've got dressed, washed my breakfast ware and made my way to Blanchardstown shopping centre in North Dublin. I've had my choice of parking spaces because nobody is up yet on this balmy Saturday morning. I get my second coffee fix in a chain-store café. The comfy seats are free and I have a moment of regret for not bringing my laptop. I could hole up here for the day and write like the stereotypical basic millennial that I am. A millennial in their natural environment, surrounded by generic over-priced coffee and free Wi-Fi.

I walk around the shops and buy two tops I don't need and some frozen yoghurt I couldn't say no to. I'll regret the dairy later.

If this day were an episode of *Sabrina the Teenage Witch*, she would be halfway down the escalator at 10.30 a.m. when she realised, 'I have said no to too many things and now I am not happy'. As I said before, Sabrina only had to have the realisation to learn the lesson. As soon as the lesson occurred to her, she became enlightened to her issue, her entire world shifted. In one episode she turned green and got warts on her nose – a caricature of an evil witch – because she was being cruel. When she realised that she had been too focused on people's appearance and had been mean to people based on their looks, the spell was reversed:, the warts disappeared and she went back to her pretty blonde self again.

I had my realisation on the escalator but the spell wasn't reversed. My friends didn't come running out of Zara and H&M. They weren't hiding behind the Leonidas chocolate kiosk or the water fountain to surprise me. The concert tickets I had said no to didn't magically appear from the sky. The lunch date didn't materialise under a white tablecloth at the bottom of the escalator, like it would have in *Sabrina*. I just realised I'd got myself into that isolated situation with all my noes and my day went on as unpopulated as it had begun.

On the escalator in Blanchardstown, I remembered a car journey from my childhood. I was famished but I didn't want to waste too much time so the Boy Housemate and I took a quick detour through the McDonald's drive-thru. As we sped along the motorway, the smell of salty carbohydrates and frying oil filling my car, I tried to steer and gobble at the same time. The Boy Housemate was horrified as I veered into the hard shoulder while I was trying to find the rogue French fries that had fallen into the bottom of the bag. The Boy Housemate shrieked, thinking I was going to crash. I over-corrected, veering into the other lane and dropping my open pot of curry sauce. I admit I shouldn't have been eating and driving, but the Boy Housemate's reaction was more dramatic than the situation called for and it was the fright rather than the fries that caused me to swerve. The point of this story is that over-correcting can be more dangerous than the original issue.

I was bored. I was experiencing a drought, just like our

little country was. I was below the activity poverty line. I had negative equity when it came to friends. This was not good. I needed to kill time because I was drowning in it. I left the shopping centre and drove from store to store, getting one ingredient for my lunch in each. I did a fifteen-kilometre round trip picking up an onion here, two bell peppers there. I drove all the way to the coast to a butcher I'd seen on Instagram just to get some turkey sausages. A girl's gotta do . . .

I came home. The water in the kettle didn't get cold all day. I kept boiling it and making coffee. It was as though the coffee bean was the only ally I had left. I cooked my dinner. I set the hob on a low level to draw out the process. It meant my stir-fry was soggy and disappointing but it seemed to hold tone with the rest of my day so I ate it. They say the best way not to feel alone when you are alone is to watch a scary movie. I found the scariest one on Netflix and watched it while I ruminated on my soggy vegetables and poor life choices. Alone.

I finish the shiny purple bag of coffee. That's eight coffees in one day. Usually I have three. Five boredom coffees is not a good sign.

Instagram is full of selfies and videos of Tay-Tay down the road in Croke Park, singing about haters or players. The air pressure is so low on this summer evening that the sound from the concert wafts up the two kilometres to my house, and I can hear a homeopathic memory of the live version. It's not so bad. I sit in the garden with the final possible cup of coffee. I hum along by myself.

I cry.

The dairy has coated my nasal cavities in phlegm and I immediately regret the frozen yoghurt. Why don't I have any tissues? Why are there no adults around? Adults always have tissues. I use toilet paper and get into bed. The hot sun has moved from the back of the house, from the kitchen where it's welcome, to my room. It's 7 p.m. and the heat is unbearable. I pull down my blinds. You could fry an egg in the heat coming off them. Maybe I should have another dinner. No, Stefanie! You are not hungry.

But I *am* hungry. I'm ravenous. Just not for food. For love. For attention. For company. Holy shit. I'm lonely. Just before I have time to get too freaked out about the reality I'm in, the Boy Housemate texts me. *Want anything from the shop?*

I've never been happier that someone's coming home. I haven't spoken to a single human all day long. I will have company and companionship and someone with whom to process the world and my feelings. I try not to gush my gratitude into a text message in case it makes him change his mind about coming home. *I finished the coffee.* I add some emojis of monkeys covering their eyes with embarrassment.

He thinks I'm embarrassed that I took the last cup. He doesn't know the real source of my shame. He doesn't know that I spent the day alone because I had said no to every offer of company and activity. He doesn't know that I texted every single person I know who lives in Dublin on that day in the hope they would take one of the heavy hours from me and share the burden of it. He doesn't know how I wandered from shop to shop buying things I didn't need in the hope that I'd feel better. He doesn't know that I had the choice of 2,000 parking spaces in the shopping centre because the other 1,999 people hadn't shown up. Even my car was alone.

I'll go to Tesco so. Purple? He loves me to Tesco and back

I respond: *Yes. Yes. Yes.*

A new era dawns. NO-ing when to say YES

38

LIKE AN ENTHUSIASTIC PENDULUM I HAVE OVER-compensated and swung too far in the other direction. I went from saying yes to everything, which was eroding my self-worth and productivity, to saying no to everything, which was eroding my self-worth and making me isolated.

This is HARD!

39

A FEW MONTHS AFTER THE DAY I SPENT ON MY OWN, I decided to run an experiment. I wanted to see if I could have an opposite experience, a morning that was intentionally dictated by other people. I wanted to relinquish control. I'd been saying so many noes, and had turned so vehemently against saying yes, I thought this experiment would open my eyes or at least make me feel good about my decision to say no. It took a lot of consideration – finding a way to do it. I didn't want to involve a friend because if I hated their plans or suggestions it'd be an unnecessary drama. I wanted a no-strings-attached fling with saying yes. I wanted a one-night stand with yes.

I considered getting on a Dublin Tour bus and letting the tourism industry dictate my day. But then I got scared that I'd offend the tour guide if I bowed out halfway through. I decided to keep it inanimate. Technology can't take offence. I handed my self-will and my morning over to the care of the men in the pedestrian lights. I decided on my way to visit Nana I would go in whichever direction the green man lit up first.

I come out of my house and turn right. I walk to the traffic lights. I want to go to Nana's house, which is a forty-five-minute walk away. It's the perfect distance on this sunny day. I have two podcasts to catch up with, and if I listen to them at one-and-a-half times the speed (as I always do) I'll have got through them by the time I reach Castleknock. I press the pedestrian crossing button and wait. The green man to my right goes green before the one ahead. So I cross to the right, seeing as it's already green and who the hell likes waiting? I walk up the road to the next set of lights. I need to go left but, again, the green man to my right goes green first so I go that way. I'm fifteen minutes into my first podcast and am now just crossing each of the streets wherever the man is green. I have relinquished control to pedestrian traffic signals.

The green light says go and I walk.

Maybe I'm starting to trust this little guy.

He's certainly got my road safety in mind so I can at least feel relatively safe.

I try not to freak out because I'm being taken away from where I want to go.

I cut the cord with my inner control freak and for the first time *maybe ever* I go with the flow.

The green man gives permission. He's not there to give direction. He says yes but it's only helpful when I already know where I'm going. I can't let people's yeses guide me. I walk along thinking about what this analogy might mean. I like analogies: they put a simple shape on some of the complexities of life. If going to Nana's house is my primary purpose, I have to say no to the green man sometimes. Whenever I'm at a crossroads, even if the pedestrian light for the other direction goes green first, or seems more appealing, I need to keep my final destination in mind. My final destination is my primary purpose, and if I go with the flow all the time, I'll end up where I don't want to be.

There are times when going for a stroll is the best thing for me, though.

Letting it all fall, taking a break, going for a stroll with no destination in mind can be relaxing. I'm learning that I don't have to be working on the pursuit of my goals to the exclusion of all else. Sometimes meeting my friends, being recreational and relaxing, is the only thing my body and mind need. There is a place for wandering and there is a place for direct, mapped routes. The green man is there for both. The green man is yes and no. Neither is better or worse: it depends on how I use them.

The terms 'introvert' and 'extrovert' didn't reach me until my teens. I got really into horoscopes and personality tests around Transition Year. It started with a yes/no quiz in the back of *Mizz* magazine and grew from there. I devoured online personality tests, filled out quizzes in the back of magazines in doctors' waiting rooms and bought books to work out who I was. That was when I first read about Karl Jung. I sort of fell off the edge of a lot of his theories, mainly because of a limited teenage vocabulary but I did understand one: he said there was no such thing as a true, pure-bred extrovert or introvert. Jung claimed that to occupy just one end of that spectrum would mean you should be in an asylum. This resonated with me.

Other quizzes had described me as being distinctly Taurean, INTJ, The Achiever or some Enneagram number I can't remember. I always zoned in on the parts that were relevant and seemed correct but part of me was always unrepresented in those descriptions. I knew that I had the capacity to be confident, bubbly and even outgoing sometimes: part of me was able to direct my energy outwards, like a ray of sun, and shine it on whoever I was interacting with. At the same time I knew I craved silence and alone time. I'd hidden that part of myself for most of my teenage years. I think I was afraid that if I admitted to enjoying being alone, I would be shunned and sentenced to solitary confinement for ever. It was confusing. I oscillated up and down this spectrum for most of my early twenties until one day at the cinema I had an epiphany.

I always get popcorn at the cinema. I love it. Even if I've

had my dinner and have sworn I'm too full for popcorn, the simple smell of it speeds up my digestive system – or maybe not but something happens and I'm hungry all over again. So, I was at the cinema with my best friend Rachel. I got popcorn and she got Maltesers. I was horrified when she suggested we mix the two: 'One is sweet and the other is savoury. You can't have both at once.'

'Sure you can,' she said, ripping open the chocolate spheres and lobbing them into my popcorn.

Two things can exist at once. Duality is OK.

I was an introvert and an extrovert and there was a word for it. *Ambivert!*

Just like the sweet and the salty, maybe I could hang out on both sides of the spectrum.

Sometimes Mam says she's still updating her information. She learned only recently not to mistake my silence for upset. But that's because I used to be dressed up as an extrovert and would be silent only when I was burned out. Now I'm often at my most content when I'm sitting inside my own brain, dangling my feet off the side of my thoughts. A while back we had a long drive together from Dublin to Westport, and over dinner Mam told me that in the past, on a journey like that, she would have been concerned there was something wrong because I was so quiet. Now she knows I'm utterly happy in those moments and she gets great peace from it.

Having people to share silent company with is the greatest gift to the introverted part of me. I doubt I'm alone in this. If I'm on my own for too long, though, the extrovert in me gets restless. It's like my personality is a riverbed. I need calm waters to feel settled, for the sand and silt to sink to the bottom. Too much action, and all of a sudden I'm disrupted with silt. Too much isolation can leave me blocked up. When it happens to the Boy Housemate – who shares my love for silence and alone time – I call it 'pent-up personality'. When it happens to me I call it neediness.

If either of us has been on our own for too long we're like dogs that need to be walked. We have all these thoughts, presentiments, theories and observations we're bursting to share with someone. It works like a dream that we understand the ebb and flow of each other so we can accommodate the various phases of our introversion/extroversion cycle. I don't take it personally when he needs to go out to dance to loud music. He doesn't take it personally when I come in from doing some front-facing extroversion work and go straight to my bed. The key is that we understand, we accept and we don't have unfair expectations.

It's hard to find a balance. I get resentful if I'm forced either to socialise too much or to spend too much time alone. I need not to overfeed one side of myself.

The Black Tie Event was a perfect example. One December I was at a fairly small Christmas gathering, surrounded by people I knew very well, loved dearly and felt totally comfortable with. I arrived and immediately got lost in conversations, catching up with people, laughing and genuinely having a good time. This is brilliant, I thought. Maybe I actually love going out again. Maybe being anti-social was a phase I grew out of. The smoked-salmon canapés, the macaroons and other food served in unnecessarily hipster containers, like Mason jars or mini-shopping trolleys, came and went, and I didn't notice because I was so lost in engaging debate.

Towards the end of the evening a friend of a friend approached me. Let's call him Gerard. 'Stefanie, great to see you. I'm heading off. Sorry we didn't get to talk.'

I smiled. 'Aw, next time I'm sure.'

'Well, actually,' said Gerard, either being polite or seeing this as a rare opportunity to catch me at a social event, 'we're having a charity fundraiser in a few weeks. X and Y will be there and we'd love to have you.'

X and Y were the two people I was sitting with in that moment. I looked at them, assessed quickly how much I was enjoying the whole evening and said, 'I'd love to.' I passed my number to Gerard and told him to get on to me with details.

Christmas passed with more entrapment under mistletoe than I would have liked. By the time January came my little flame was extinguished to an ember. The text arrived on a Thursday as I sat drinking coffee with the Boy Housemate. Maybe we were sitting in silence, maybe we were working out one of our random musings, like why we fill an online shopping cart with clothes but when they charge five euros for delivery we change our minds. *See you Saturday, it's black tie.*

Gerard's text was like a punch in the neck. Who the hell throws a black-tie event at someone three days before go-time? That's a full-on sartorial commitment. My hackles were up. I immediately regretted saying I would go. I hated extroverted Stefanie for sentencing introverted Stefanie to an evening of black-tie small-talk. I had no memory of ever thinking this was a good idea.

The day arrived and all I wanted to do was stay in my house and fill myself with hot drinks and terrestrial television. However, Stefanie Preissner is nothing if not dependable. If I say I'll do something I'll go out of my way to do it. I refuse ever to be described as unreliable or flaky. So, like a good Cinderella, I went to the ball.

When I got there I was immediately greeted by a cluster of Karen Millen- and Ted Baker-clad women who were delighted to see me. I was delighted to see them, too, but I couldn't find my words. It was as though my vocabulary allowance for the day had been revoked. I was like the Little Mermaid who gets to walk on land but she has to trade in her voice. I knew that to get through the event I would have to regulate my environment.

You'll often see me on my own in a corner at a party. I'm just refuelling, like those electric cars at the side of the road. People at the event must have thought I had some digestive issues, or maybe I was sick or even pregnant. I would manage four to six minutes of good-quality chit-chat before I'd have to excuse myself and go to the bathroom. There, I would put down the toilet lid and sit for fifteen minutes, just gathering myself and my strength before heading out into the rough waters of social etiquette again. It sounds like I'm crazy, I know.

Now it was up to me to work out when and why I would suddenly switch from one to the other.

For a while I felt like a crazy person. I googled terms like 'schizophrenic' and 'bipolar' to try to understand why one day I would wake up excited to meet friends in a café and the next day I'd be trying to cough up a lung as an excuse to get out of a lunch date. I could tolerate and even enjoy spontaneity and novelty in certain environments.

Today I'm feeling very chirpy, pleasant and social. It's Monday and I'm meeting my friend for her birthday. I'm taking her for lunch because I didn't attend her party on Saturday night. I can't wait to see her and chat and get all the stories from her. In this moment, I can't remember what anti-social Stefanie feels like. I can't conjure up the true feeling of discomfort, anxiety and unease I feel. Maybe it's an evolutionary protection thing, like women forget the true pain of childbirth. Who knows?

When I'm in my extroverted phases I need to be really careful. I always want to say, 'Yes!' to offers made to me on those days. But I've learned to say, 'Can you leave that with me?' so I don't throw introvert Stefanie under the bus or let people down. I call up my most introverted day and think, Would I be able to do what is being asked of me on that day? If it's a yes, I'll generally say yes. I mean, even at my quietest I can bring someone to the airport or buy groceries for Nana, or do an interview via email.

I had to dig deep to understand the change in myself. I would get so frustrated when an invitation I wanted, theoretically, to accept would come in yet I knew it was outside my capacities. Why was I like this? Why could I be super-chatty and 'on', revelling in attention on one day and the next I'm hiding in a toilet cubicle in a four-star hotel watching ASMR videos on YouTube to calm myself?

I started to wonder if it was my hormones. As I began to

take note of the changes, I realised that being in the company of the right people had an awful lot to do with it. I become drained by certain types of people and environments very quickly. Some places, like loud restaurants or cafés, any kind of nightclub, festivals, sports events or concerts are incredibly exigent. In those environments all of my senses are attacked. It's too bright, too loud, too smelly, too squished. All of that, coupled with company who require me to drive a conversation is too much. I try to control as many of those factors as I can. It's probably the reason I have my 'usuals'. These are places, food orders and preferences that I return to time and time again. If someone I'm at ease with suggests somewhere new I'll usually trust them and take a chance, but if I'm meeting someone I don't know, I'll go to my 'usuals'.

Rachel gave me the push to saying my first ongoing no. It's one I seem to have to say again and again. I didn't realise I had to tackle it until Rachel pointed it out. If anyone else had brought it to my attention I would have been furious. Rachel is great at highlighting things in a kind, non-judgemental, shame-free way. This was exactly the tone she took when delivering the frightening news that I needed to start saying no to the wily, coarse chin hair I have that pops up, fully grown sometimes. I pluck or wax it. I track it and search for it in mirrors across the world. The lighting in some store changing rooms is brutal. It doesn't flatter *anyone* but it does shed a fluorescent beacon on my chin hair. Rachel and I have christened it Doris after Doris Day. I have started saying no to Doris every time she appears. If all else fails and I can't say no to anything else, I'll always have a Tweezerman ready to say no to Doris. She is my most consistent no.

I continue to work on finding out how to set my priorities. I play around with schedules and make lists in order of descending importance to help me reject the things I don't need. I've said no to outright noes. I've said no to being definitive. If I just said a blanket no to everything, like I had been doing, I would quickly become someone who declines every offer or request for her time. Anyone can do that. They're called hermits, recluses and loners. I've seen them on American reality TV, crushed by towers of sixty-year-old newspapers, or trapped in the maze of loneliness that has become their home.

Yes, I want to achieve all the things on my list. Yes, I want to be productive and prolific. Yes, I want to protect myself from the crippling anxiety I feel when I'm forced into social situations. No, I don't want to end up alone, friendless and with only fictitious experiences in my memories. So I am now on my quest to know when to say yes.

40

SOME PEOPLE LOVE A GOOD WEDDING. TO OTHERS they can be overwhelming. I fall into this latter category. Being in a crowd of people who want to 'chat' to each other turns me into a version of Sandra Bullock in *Gravity*. *Waaaay* beyond sky high. The anxiety rockets to orbital levels, making me concerned about the most random things. It's not just 'Oh, crap, how am I going to make small-talk with this woman?' It could be as bizarre and crippling as 'Oh, God, people want to make conversation. *Where is my birth certificate? I haven't seen it in years.*' Fears about locking hall doors and unplugging the iron are the types of curious fear that fill me when I'm forced to be in a crowd of people who want to chit-chat. It's not that I'm rude or unfriendly, it's just that I don't understand why I need to know how many brothers you have, where you're from or how you know our shared friend.

Someone has decided to unite with their other half and, because of that, I'm down €175! That's only the *basic* fine. That's a cheap outfit, a measly gift, shared accommodation and those gel insoles that make high heels bearable. If I want to go alone and be branded 'a little bit stingy' that's the fine. If I get involved in all possible stages of their event, that fine can be driven closer to a thousand euro. With hen parties, engagement parties, hotel stays, group activities, dresses, make-up, hair and endless cocktails, you'd be sensible to look at taking out a Credit Union loan. For many, other people's weddings mean forgoing a holiday on their own terms.

At a wedding, you're never going to see most of those people again until a significant birthday or a funeral. I don't have the natural instinct to make conversation so my questions, instead of appearing light, casual and friendly, are received more as inquisitions. A small-talk tête-à-tête with me at a wedding can make someone feel like they've been captured by a terrorist and interrogated over the canapés. It's even worse when you're eventually permitted to stop milling around. Then you're expected to do the same thing *while seated*. This is even more stressful. Most Irish weddings have adopted the 'large round table' design. There are usually eight to ten people at each table. That's four or five couples or a mix of couples and singles. Your table is often one of many, scattered around a function room. This means you're surrounded by people on all sides.

I am never more uncomfortable than when I know there are people on all sides of me. They can come from anywhere and catch you off guard with a question or a greeting, giving you no time to prepare your socially acceptable smile. So you sit there, the women trying to avoid the bread rolls and the men trying not to be caught looking for an escape route.

It's as simple as this: weddings are soup and I am a fork. We are incompatible. I have learned in the last few years not to entertain the idea of attending one. I can protect myself from weeks of turmoil by saying no from the get-go. I never really felt guilty for drawing this boundary.

Then Rachel got engaged.

I know it means a lot to Rachel that I attend her wedding. They say you can tell what gift to get a person by taking note of the gifts they give to other people. If I apply this logic to Rachel, showing up at her wedding would be the greatest gift: Rachel makes *such* an effort to show up for other people.

Showing up means I'd be prioritising my friendship over my comfort zone. It means saying yes to something I regularly say no to. The context is everything. I had learned that making a habit of saying no doesn't end well. It means a lot to me to be loyal, and to be a good friend – the rules from primary school have taken root. Rachel doesn't expect anything of me other than to be her friend. I don't have to fix her problems, look a certain way, be the life and soul of the party. I just have to be there, and there I will be. I will enjoy being present for my friend more than I would enjoy my solitude on that day. So I said yes.

I try to say yes to people I love more often than no. I'm relearning how to say yes. Sometimes I'm asked to speak at events, to groups of young people, to comment on something that is happening in the country, and even though I get riddled with anxiety about doing it, I recognise that the cause is greater than my comfort in that moment. It's not about me at all. I'm getting better at not shouting, 'No!' and running away.

If I say yes to something I have to forget that saying no was ever an option. I fully commit to my yes. At Rachel's wedding I will be fully there. I will enjoy every minute, and when it gets to the point in the night when I'm uncomfortable, I'll go to bed. I'll be gracious and honoured to be there. After all, it's gorgeous that someone wants me around on the happiest day of their life so far. I won't have to pretend to enjoy this one, although I'm *very* good at pretending. And I give acting classes if you, too, have to go to something you don't want to. Find me on Twitter or Instagram. I'll sort you out.

Twitter: @stefpreissner

Instagram: stefaniepreissner

41

WHEN I LOOK AT MY FUTURE, I LOOK TO MY NANA. She's the future. I want my life to look something like this.

I am ninety. The walls of my hallway are adorned with awards and accolades from my writing career, mainly TV, but I dabbled in film. I had one great acting role, then went into politics for a while and did something great for the world. There's a framed letter that explains I've been nominated for an Emmy and a list of rules of how to proceed:

» How to get a designer to style me.

⇸ What I am allowed to say in my acceptance speech.

⇸ What I am NOT allowed to say in my acceptance speech.

⇸ What shoes and clothes I should wear.

⇸ How to lose graciously.

I didn't win the Emmy but it's the nomination that counts, right? That's on one side of the imaginary hallway in the house I live in now that I'm ninety. On the other wall are photographs, all taken in the same sunny house. A house I own in Hawaii. Kona, Kailua, Hawaii. It's got this outdoor seating area, unvarnished wood and big soft cushions on a big square seat. Two grandchildren, one boy, one younger girl, can chart their growth through how many cushions they had to stack to climb onto the edge of the veranda to watch the sunsets with us. 'Us' is me and my husband and our two sons. Each married. Each the father of one of those grandkids. I have grey hair, and it suits me the way it suits Meryl Streep, Maggie Smith or Olwen Fouéré. I am happy to say I have had no facial plastic surgery and I have retained good elasticity in the skin. I am lean, but I don't look like those old people who do yoga and resemble greyhounds. That's the hallway of my house. My house, in Dublin.

The house is bright and airy and the ceilings go up for miles. There are two sofas. One looks like it hasn't ever been sat in. But one half of the other sofa looks like a boulder has been resting there since time began. That's where my husband sits.

Well, he's ninety-four so he mainly sleeps. Upstairs, the rooms where our sons used to sleep have been turned elegantly into guest rooms. The master bedroom was upstairs until we got an extension to spare ourselves the journey in our later years.

I tend the garden myself. It's my pride and joy. It's got all sorts of flowers whose names I know how to pronounce, and I know their Latin names, too, and how often you have to water them. I have a book club of lovely women who come to my house. When it's cold we take our weekly book to the poly-tunnel and drink coffee. I'm an avid poker player. I win money every week on top of my hefty pension so I'm minted. I have a Land Rover outside and I'm like Queen Elizabeth II driving around in it.

I am still a contributor to *The Cutting Edge*. He's a hundred-and-ten now and showing no signs of stopping. Ryan Tubridy is still hosting *The Late Late Show*. Simon Harris is the leader of our country and we do lunch. One Direction are doing a revival tour. I go to the concert with the Boy Housemate, for nostalgia's sake. We don't have to travel far because teleportation has been invented for the wealthy so we pool our bitcoin and use that to deliver us right to our seats. All of our friends are there, waiting for us. Some are in two places at once because you can do that through your phone.

Rachel, my best friend, and I meet for lunch every second day – it's no biggie because flights to New York take twenty minutes and it's post-terrorism so security isn't even a thing. We try everything on the menu in a restaurant, then move on to the next. We've been doing this for thirty years. Rachel writes reviews of the places so we mainly eat for free.

I am surrounded by people I love, showering them with attention, generosity and kindness. My grandkids are obsessed with me, and I them. They often come with me for lunch. I have great health and fabulous teeth. I never look off trend, and young people still see me as a style icon. My opinions and views are not outdated. I know all the new bands, new acronyms, new gadgets, actors and TV shows. I have organised several of my friends' daughters' weddings, and am constantly asked to write speeches. My Ted talk is the most attended and viewed ever.

It's my ninety-first birthday. I didn't celebrate my ninetieth because I was getting my blood transfused with my granddaughter's. It's the new way to keep people alive. To thank her, I took her to the Natural History Museum. She was fascinated by the bees, the plastic straws and a funny display of old running shoes. She couldn't get her head around the concept that people used to travel places on foot.

I've decided to have my ninety-first birthday party in the Starbucks Church. It's a steal. For 12,000 bitcoin Google will organise a bespoke event inspired by your average dreams with data gathered through their dream-app and augmented by your most-viewed Pinterest boards. Blue Ivy Carter is going to sing me a song while I blow out ninety-one candles lit by the Olympic Flame, which the two rowers from Cork will carry from Greece for me.

Hang on a second – I've lost the run of myself here. I would never, ever want a giant ninety-first birthday party with a lot of people and a Beyoncé relative singing to me. As soon as that was suggested to me I would have said no. So scrap all that. I'm ageing quietly and gracefully.

Actually, I would probably have said no to keeping up with TV shows and actors too: I don't like watching new TV shows so I'm probably still watching the US version of *The Office* on an ancient DVD player and mourning the passing of Steve Carell.

There probably wouldn't be very many people at that ninety-first party because I don't really feel the need to make new friends, or find myself in situations with a lot of new people around. So it's likely that it's just me and the Boy Housemate, my kids and grandkids. But how am I meant to get kids and grandkids if I keep saying no to all the situations that lead to kids and grandkids?

Light-bulb moment happening live as I type. Let's look at all the things I've planned for my future and how they're not possible because of the uncompromising and non-negotiable way I'm living my life.

Hallway with awards and accolades.

I say no to having excess stuff hanging on my walls because it looks messy. I haven't been nominated for too many awards, but the ones I have been, I haven't attended the ceremonies because I say no to evening events and anything with more than two people. So that would never happen.

Photos of house in Hawaii.

It takes *soooo* long to get to Hawaii, and I tend to say no to travelling unless it's absolutely necessary. I can't see this ever being something I would actually do. Eleven hours from Dublin to Los Angeles, and then a lay-over? I mean, come on. I could skip the lay-over but I'd be on edge for the whole flight wondering if I'd make my connecting flight in LAX, which is an incredibly onerous airport to navigate. I've just checked and you can fly to Hawaii via San Francisco but I reckon that's more of the same. People think Hawaii is a hop, skip and a jump from LAX but it's not. It's another six or seven hours. So, all in all, you're talking a full day's travelling. Put jet-lag on top of that, and the potential to be travelling with grandchildren . . . No way. Sure the Aran Islands are basically Hawaii if it's sunny. And there's always the Canary Islands.

I have grey hair.

I spend inordinate amounts of money making sure this never happens. So why in my fantasy do I have grey hair? I have combed through my hair with tweezers, selecting the grey ones for eradication to postpone my trip to Siobhan in Darcy's hair salon. This fantasy Stefanie is a totally different person from me.

House in Dublin with tended garden.

I can't garden! What was I thinking? There's way too much out of my control in a garden. I once spent a whole summer planting lettuces and flowers and watering them, tending them. Then snails came along and ate the bloody lettuces, there was biblical rain, which drowned my flowers, and I spend most of August drowsy from hay fever tablets. The whole thing was a f**king disaster. I am terrible at gardening and I do not enjoy it. Why does this feature in my ideal future?

I host a book club?

I continually say no to group activities and invitations to be in book clubs. When does this change in the next sixty years? Does it? And how?

Boys' rooms changed to guest rooms upstairs.

If I ever had kids, and I don't see how that would be possible based on many of my noes, I would never change their rooms into anything after they had left. It's just not who I am as a person.

Surrounded by people.

No, no, no, please don't make me go.

Fabulous teeth.

I put off my dental appointments too much for this ever to be a reality. But it is something I want for my life.

Never looking off-trend.

Unlikely – I guffaw at people who fall victim to fashion slavery. I wonder why that's something I aspire to when I'm ninety.

New bands and acronyms, organising weddings, giving a Ted talk, attending a One Direction concert and augmenting my blood to keep me young.

There are all the things that, if proposed to me today, I would scream, 'No!' at and run as fast as I could in the opposite direction. I would love to be able to meet Rachel in a different lunch place every day – but I love habit and sameness. Am I ever going to grow out of these things? I'm thirty now so I'm fairly set in my ways and nothing is going to change unless I change. All the noes I say on a daily basis are not taking me to the life I am dreaming for myself. WTF? Also, a husband. *Where is the Boy Housemate in all this?* He cannot not be part of my future. That's not a world I want to live in.

Writing these last few paragraphs has given me a pain in my stomach. I need to go and lie down in a foetal curl.

I'm back. I lay like a foetus and listened to some Nickelback and now I have some perspective that things could be worse.

If I say no to everything that scares me, I'd never do anything. Ever. If I live my life saying no to everything I don't want to do, with no compromise, I'm going to end up dying alone in a cave. I wouldn't get up in the morning. I'd watch reruns of *Friends* and *The Office* all day while having Nando's and Sprout deliver food to me. I would run out of money. I would probably ask the Boy Housemate to bankroll me for a while. This would put a strain on our relationship to the point where he would eventually have to leave me. Then I would move on to other friends and family to bankroll me until no one wanted to speak to me, and Nando's and Sprout stopped answering my calls and Instagram messages.

Soon after that, I'd get hungry and that would be the only thing forcing me to leave my house. My phone battery would die because my agents and editors and producers would be blowing up my phone looking for my work. I'd steal food and be chased by the police. I'd return home under the cover of darkness only to realise the keys no longer fit because the locks have been changed. My house has been repossessed. I'd board a night train to Mitchelstown and live in the caves there, eating rats and entertaining myself with stories of my past. Maybe I'd carry a magazine with me on the cover as ID so people would know that, for a moment, I was worth putting on a magazine cover. I'd die alone.

In the above example, I say no to absolutely everything I don't want to do. And I die alone in a cave. This is my way of proving I'm not as uncompromising as I think. I do say yes to lots of things that I would rather say no to. It takes a while to discern the things that are worth saying yes to even if I don't want to. I'm still working on it and I often get it wrong.

There are things I say yes to because I want to be the kind of person who does those things.

Maybe I'm being too hard on myself. There are, in my defence, many things I've said yes to. Perhaps I just focus on the noes because they protect me.

If I start to say yes to some of the things that scare me, maybe one day my ideal future will look like how I imagine it. If I keep saying no to everything, it won't play out well. I hate caves and darkness. I like having my people around me.

Saying yes to university might be a little regret of mine, but it was the base camp for where I've gone since. Even Shakespeare in the Park was worth saying yes to because it showed me I couldn't stick at the acting game full-time any more. Hang on . . . am I having some kind of spiritual awakening here? You know those moments where your real-life experiences make you have a realisation that is a cliché and then you feel kind of stupid for being so basic because the lesson was there all along; on Instagram, on decals above people's beds, tattooed onto people, on every motivational website ever –

No regrets. Everything that has happened has made you who you are.

Jesus.

It's time to build a new fantasy – a fantasy of what I actually want, what I want to say yes to. I know I will consistently say yes to the people who matter, the people I love. I want to bring to every relationship – family, work, romantic and friendship – a happy Stefanie, who is stable and happy, and can make healthy decisions. I'll never say no to Nana, my mother, or my friends. I love being loyal and helpful too much for that. I love rules too much not to pay my bills, so I can be sure that I won't get into debt. If I'm not going into overdraft, it's sort of safe to fantasise that I'll have a house, the same one for a long time, and it will be clean and clutter-free.

My people are generous and kind; they like to give me presents. I can say no when I have the option but I would never hand back an unsolicited present and, in these social-media times, re-gifting is dangerous. So I will say yes to the scented candles, and the framed pictures, the novelty cushions and all of the books. My house will be tidy but lived in.

Sometimes, maybe, I'll have a birthday party. A small one. There will be no speeches or special guests. No Blue Ivy or One Direction. There'll be a series of one-on-one lunches spread out over the course of a month with the people who want to celebrate my birthday.

I think about Nana. I think about all the noes and yeses she has said. She's the strongest woman I know, and at an age at which she doesn't have time to waste on being uncomfortable or not enjoying something. She said no to the idea that women should avoid university. She said yes to moving to Dublin to study chemistry and pharmacy when that was a male-dominated field. She said yes to getting married, yes to having multiple children, yes to cruises and parties and the cinema.

She tells stories of Mediterranean cruises: each time they docked at a port she would find a pub, place my grandfather in it, and go exploring on her own or with her best friend Nuala, unencumbered by her incurious husband. She has endless tales of day adventures to Dún Laoghaire or Dalkey, just to see the sea. She talks of being in London with no money because she spent her daily allowance on a Knickerbocker Glory. She's said yes to everything she was offered and now, in her slowed-down, scaled-back old age, she can pass four hours with just her memories of those times. Perhaps saying yes to things is just that: it's banking memories, creating stories for when you can no longer say yes. That's a sobering thought.

So I'm in my future house, and my magazines are not my only form of identification. They're kept in drawers with maybe one or two, framed for me as gifts, displayed on the walls. It's less *Whatever Happened to Baby Jane?* that way. My hair is still impeccably dark. Siobhan still does my cut and colour in D'Arcy's. It's my one lasting vanity. On the walls there are photos of children, a husband and grandchildren. But we're in a house on a Canary Island, which is only four hours away and Ryanair fly there. There is a granny flat where The Boy Housemate stays when he can. I have family and friends I enjoy.

The holiday photos in this permutation of my fantasy are a little hazier. I can't see the faces of my husband or future family. Maybe a nuclear family won't materialise – but it won't be because I've said no to meeting new people. I've met a ferocious number of new people in the last three years, mainly through my job. I shouldn't be so hard on myself for not being as social as I feel people expect me to be. I'm doing great. Even if that family in the photos never happens, I get great comfort from the family I have now, my friends and their babies, Nana, Mam, my cousins and their kids, and as I age they will still be there. I don't have to be afraid.

I've said yes to things that are difficult for me:

» Contributing to political commentary panels on TV and radio when I have felt completely unqualified.

» Having my photo taken with only one piece of clothing on.

» Losing 150 pounds of weight.

» Attending the 30 under 30 awards.

» Going to a Christmas party for a newspaper I contribute to.

- → Going to group lunches where I know only two people.

- → Being a make-up model for my cousin Sarah.

- → Taking Nana to every appointment she asks me to take her to.

- → Babysitting other people's kids.

- → And I am making a commitment right now to saying yes to.

- → Attending Rachel's 2019 wedding.

- → Going on *The Graham Norton Show* if they ever ask me.

- → Running for President of Ireland at some point, LOL.

- → Any opportunity that might lead to me having a show on US television.

- → Any chance at making memories in the sun with my family .

I take great comfort from knowing I can say no, if I want to. There's a glorious warmth that comes with knowing I will never have to do a bungee jump or a hen party. It makes me feel like I can stand in a power pose, fully straight with my shoulders back and my hands on my hips. I imagine all the future requests or expectations flying at me – right towards my heart. Knowing I can say no is a powerful shield. The requests bounce off my torso with comic-book graphics.

Walk the Camino! POW – NO! The request flies across the room and shatters into a billion pieces. Let your hair down! NO! BAM! It explodes with the power of my 'No!' I never have to go to anything where 'letting your hair down' is on the agenda. It's my life, my path, my journey. It's my blank canvas to paint however I goddamn choose. If I want to, I can paint the whole thing black. I can use wax or paint or pencil or nail varnish. I can paint it all or I can just colour it all in white crayon and put one tiny dot in the corner. A tiny dot. A full stop. IT'S MY PAINTING. It's my life. I can do what I want. It's great to know that in saying yes to some things, loosening my grip, I am not waiving my right to choice: I am not disqualifying myself from ever saying no again.

Saying no to things that are not good for you is one thing, but saying no to things that you're just afraid of or uncomfortable with can hold you back. Saying yes makes a life.

If I had said no to everything that I wanted to say no to that summer in Barcelona, I wouldn't have learned how my gut feels when I know I'm in danger. I wouldn't have the stories to tell. I wouldn't be able to connect with people who also have horror stories of student holidays. I wouldn't have a healthy fear of Welsh men on cocaine.

Nana sits in her chair in the corner of her living room. I try to visit when no one else is there. That's not because I don't like my family – to the contrary, we get on great. I simply think it's better for us to spread ourselves across Nana's week, like Nutella on the smooth side of a Ryvita cracker. If you spread it on the bumpy side, it all clumps into the concave bits and you get some dry, boring sections with none of the sweetness. I want Nana to have a layer of sweetness across her whole week.

You can hear the TV blaring before you turn the key in the door. The front of the house is mainly glass, that old glass with little circle swirls all over it, as if the end of a wine bottle was pressed into it before it was solid. When she hears the door close, there's a shuffle and the volume on the TV goes down. She used to have the volume set always to 31, but in the last few years that's changed. It started with her saying, 'That Graham Norton talks fierce low,' before reaching for the remote to increase it 34. Then it was *The Crown*: apparently the Queen is 'too polite to speak up' and the remote brought her close to 40. Now the volume can get as high as 48 and I frequently catch Nana's eyes following my lips when I speak to her. She's losing her hearing but she doesn't want to talk about it. So we don't mention it. The TV goes off when I come in. She puts the kettle on because ''tis good for me to be moving'.

When I watch movies, old people are always rendered as broken records: they have lived lives but are reduced to three anecdotes. They tell the same three stories on repeat, boring the family who have to sit through 'the time I met the president' over and over.

Nana has no such affliction. To this day, she tells stories I haven't heard before. Crazy, wild stories that you can't believe she's been sitting on for all these years. She still cracks herself up, and me. She tells stories of saving her money and pooling it with her friend to buy an iced bun on Merrion Square.

She talks about the price of her wedding: two shillings and sixpence. As a kid, the craziest prank she ever pulled was knocking on a stranger's door and asking for a glass of water. I told her we used to knock on doors and run away. She said that was for wimps and started cackling with laughter.

Nana found the body of a tenant who had committed suicide. She was one of the first chemists in Dublin who distributed methadone to heroin addicts. She was kind, progressive and thoughtful. Nana has years and years of memories that fill weeks of chats over cups of tea. They seem to be endless. As I sit with her, listening to another new story, I wonder about my life. With her multiple hip replacements, and the other ailments that go with old age, her ninety years force her to say no to many of life's offerings now. But all the yeses she has said in her life are wrapped around her like an experiential pass-the-parcel. You peel back one story layer and there is another, then another and another. It goes on for ever because of the yeses she has said. Her yeses from the past mean that the noes in her present aren't so devastating.

If I keep saying no to everything I'll have no more stories to tell. I'll just be sitting on my own, in my house, with a phenomenal capacity to say no . . . but nothing else.

Saying yes builds a life.

I love black and white. I love the contrast of yin and yang. I love the clean lines and clear borders of IKEA. I love traffic junctions with filter lights. I love food packages that give detailed nutritional information, including what exactly a portion is. I love menus with pictures of what a dish will look like so you know what you're ordering, more so when restaurants put photos of their dishes on Instagram so you can do some research. I love an itinerary. I love the graphic designer who invented the exit sign. The three little icons are so clear and useful. I love clothing that comes with precise cleaning instructions. I love wrapping a present when the design on the two edges of the wrapping paper lines up perfectly. I love standing in Tower Bay on Portrane's coast, looking across to Lambay Island and seeing the detail of what's going on. I love things that are clear and simple. Having definitive statements makes me feel safe.

I love having a label. Maybe it's because all my life I've been double-barrelled: I'm German-Irish. I was born on 21 April so I'm an Aries-Taurus cuspian. I am an extroverted-introvert or an ambivert. I can write with both of my hands. I look for definitive things to attach to myself so I feel secure in my identity. But those things are not useful for ever. I have to let go of definitive statements because they keep me trapped. Life is about compromise. If I only say yes I will be stifled and resentful; if I only say no I will be lonely and disloyal. I hate grey areas but that's where life happens.

I love Oprah.

I love how honest she is and how she tries to be positive even when she's not feeling great. She taught me that gratitude is the key to most problems. I'm starting to see that the grey area of life is a blessing and a privilege for which I should be incredibly grateful. I am grateful that I have a choice. I'm not forced to say yes or no. I have options. I am paralytically indecisive so it's not always the most comfortable place to be but wouldn't it be so much worse if all of my decisions were made for me and I wasn't allowed autonomy? I have freedom, and freedom is power.

I have the power to decide what I do without pressure or threat from the people in my life.

I might still say yes to things that I regret but at least I know that I could have said no and that makes it much more tolerable. I'm getting better at saying no because I now know that I can. I can say no and still be lovable, and worthy, and accepted. I have learned that by knowing myself and my personality type, and accepting them.

Each step on my journey has led me to the next, and even though some were difficult, I learned something along the way.

By not trying to be 'positive vibes only', I realised I was unhappy as a people-pleaser.

Even though people were pleased with me, I was not happy.

By accepting that I wasn't happy, I learned that I had to change something.

By looking at what needed to change I discovered who I am, what my personality is.

By accepting that that was who I really am, even though I would have preferred to 'build a different bear', I was able to stop putting myself in situations that didn't suit me.

By changing that habit I realised I didn't know who I am: all the years of saying yes had dulled my taste-buds to what I actually liked.

By being afraid to go back to being a people-pleaser, I said no to too many things. I'm grateful for this because it showed me that I needed to stick my head out of my shell and come back into the world.

Right now I'm still in the testing phase. I think you stay in it for a long time. It's life. Life is about trying things out, keeping what works and discarding the rest. I know that weddings and Arcade Fire concerts are a big fat no, but lunches and friendships and family and work are so important that I can override my discomfort because I know who I am and what my primary purposes in life are.

But the biggest thing I've learned is about power. I have the power and I won't give it away. I won't put Little Stef into situations where she can't be heard or where she's afraid. I keep telling her what I've learned along the way: *You can say no.*

And sometimes I do.

And sometimes I say yes.

Because life's all about options.

Maybe now I'll die happy.

Well, actually, I can't control how I die.

But I can control how I live. So make it: Maybe that way I'll live happy.

Yes.

AckNOwledgements

THANK YOU.

No.

Thank YOU!

Massive thank you to the Boy Housemate for being my brother, my 'husband' and my soul-mate. Thank you to him for designing the cover and for telling me 'No!' every time I walk out of my room in an outfit I think is acceptable as formal wear.

Thank you to Mam, for being patient and tolerant and just a great laugh.

Thanks to Nana, for showing me that even if you say no, the people who care won't love you any less.

Thanks to Lorcan and Aileen, Clara and Terry.

Thanks to everyone in Hachette, for sticking with me through title changes, breakdowns and for stopping me running away.

Thanks to Jasmine, my agent, who is the person I need most when I've failed to say no.

Thank you to Arianna Huffington, for being so kind as to blurb the book, and Matthew Carnahan for being a helpful genius.

Thanks to Bank of Ireland for saying no to that overdraft I wanted.

Thank you to everyone who bought my last book – it's because of you I could write this one.

Thanks to Karl Henry, Gina Moxley, Sam Ford, Jessie Bolger, Maria Walsh, Patrick Freyne, Doireann Garrihy and Terry Prone for their contribution and insight into NO at work. My editors said no to including some of them but they were nevertheless helpful.

Thank you to Rachel, for being the sister I need but don't have, and for trudging the road of life with me, for helping me see my blind spots and for being the best cheerleader a girl could ask for. For teaching me how to say no but, more importantly, for giving me the opportunity to say yes.

WHY CAN'T EVERYTHING JUST
STAY THE SAME?
»–> AND OTHER THINGS I SHOUT WHEN I CAN'T COPE

'WITTY ... AND WRITTEN
WITH REAL HEART'
THE SUNDAY TIMES

'HONEST, WITTY
AND POIGNANT
OBSERVATIONS ON LIFE'
AMY HUBERMAN

'LASHINGS OF SUBTLE WIT
AND WISDOM'
SUNDAY INDEPENDENT

STEFANIE PREISSNER

As a child, being in new places made Stefanie Preissner ill, which is why her family holidayed in the same apartment on the same island off the Spanish coast for nine years in a row. And why, at Christmas, she wrote lengthy letters to Santa (note: letters, plural) begging him not to bring any surprises. Change was the enemy. But, as it turns out, one Stefanie hasn't been able to avoid. And, in spite of herself, one she has sometimes invited into her life.

In her first book, Stefanie looks at the ways in which her life has changed. From birthdays, friendships and how she celebrates the festive season, to social media (no FOMO here), the importance of asking WWNSD? (What Would Nicole Scherzinger Do?) when faced with big decisions, and her career as a writer, *Why Can't Everything Just Stay the Same?* is the hilarious and honest account of one woman's journey to and through adulthood, coping (sort of) with the terror, inevitability and beauty of change.

Also available as an ebook